BORROWED NAME

O.Dakova

Table of Contents:

Introduction

In this book, I wanted to write about important, in my opinion, aspects of our lives and invite you, my dear readers, to also think about them and draw your own conclusions. The main aspects discussed in this book is man, his role in life and his relationship with the world, society and himself. The limitless resourcefulness and intelligence of man, his incredible abilities to dream and make dreams come true made man so powerful on this planet that he became the master of this world or, let's say, like God. Everything he created, invented and did is simply amazing. Beautiful cities with wonderful architecture, amazing and reliable cars and planes, space rockets, various types of art, music that touches and shakes the hearts - all this is made by man. And now people, thanks to the human mind, live in such comfort and convenience that none of the previous generations could even dream of. But he, man, so skillfully and beautifully woven by nature and the forces of the Universe, possessing incredible ingenuity, does not always manifest himself in this world as he should. For some reason he does not feel happy and satisfied with his life. The lack of a sense of happiness pushes him onto the path of destruction, war and hatred. To do this, he also creates wise and ingenious weapons to destroy people he dislikes and life around him. The only thing man could not create, as I think, is an internal stable peace within himself. Many philosophical and spiritual teachings say that a person needs to learn to control his inner feelings and desires and bring them to a state of peace and harmony. If he cannot do this, being overwhelmed by the rage and hatred raging within him, a person loses the correct idea of himself and the world, and, thereby, destroys both himself and the world around him. Two Biblical quotations, sayings of Moses and Jesus Christ, suggest that people have a distorted view of both themselves and the world. And this is the reason that creates so much troubles and sufferings in their lives. Here they are:

"Until this day the Lord (God) has not given you the heart to understand, eyes to see and ears to hear". (Deuteronomy 29-4);

"This is why I speak to them in parables: Though seeing, they do not see, though hearing, they do not hear or understand." (Matthew: 13-13).

At first glance, it seems, these words have nothing to do with us. We all are well educated and understand everything correctly. This could only be said about our ancestors. They did not see, hear and understand. But difficult situations in the world prompted me to take a closer look at these statements, and I drew some conclusions about them. They express only my personal opinions on all issues discussed in this book. I do not want or seek to impose my understanding of things on anyone, but simply want to invite everyone to also think about the main issues raised in this book. Thank you! And happy reading!!!

Can these statements be true for us?

Shown above phrases belong to two famous spiritual leaders - Moses and Jesus Christ. So, I think, it would be better to pay more attention to that what these great people say. Note: The time difference between the lives of Moses and Jesus Christ is about several thousand years. That is, for thousands of years from the time of Moses to the time of Jesus Christ, people of Israel, as stated in the Bible, were still not able to see, hear and understand Reality correctly. Moses was the most prominent spiritual leader of Israel. Many Israelis still live by his commandments to this days.

There is no need to introduce Jesus Christ. The whole world knows him. He healed the incurable, restored sight to the blind, hearing to the deaf, and raised the dead. His teaching is alive and active to this day. If both of these statements are true, then this means that the Israelis from Moses to Jesus Christ for thousands of years remained blind, deaf and did not have a correct understanding of Reality.

Moses believed that the only way to help his people gain "eyes that see, ears that hear, and minds that understand" was to make a covenant with God, promising to live only by His laws and not deviate from them in any way. The Israelis concluded such a covenant under his leadership several times but, unfortunately, these attempts were not crowned with success. So, thousands of years after Moses, Jesus Christ said about these same people the same thing that Moses said in his time:

"Through seeing, they do not see; through hearing, they do not hear and do not understand."

The Israelis, despite their great desire to see, hear and understand Reality correctly, remained in the time of Jesus Christ as blind, deaf and without correct understanding as they were in the time of Moses. The Israelis did not believe in man-made gods from wood or gold, as most other nations at that time did. They believed in the Living God. During the exodus from Egyptian slavery, they saw with their own eyes the most incredible miracles performed by God through Moses. They saw how the Egyptian rivers were filled with blood, all the Egyptian firstborns died in one night, and the waters of the Red Sea parted before them, opening up a way out of the land of slavery. The Israelis loved and stood in awe of God and were afraid to break His commandments. But despite all their love for God, in the time of Jesus Christ they were as blind, deaf and without a correct understanding of Reality as in the time of Moses.

In this case, the question naturally arises: what about the followers of Jesus Christ and us, living today? Do we see, hear and understand the world we live in correctly? Can we also be blind and deaf? One day, holding my attention on these phrases, I decided to take a deeper look at the history of mankind. It turned out that it is not so difficult to find in history many well-known examples of the errors of mankind literally in everything. Our ancestors, for example, lived for tens thousands of years in delusion about the shape of the Earth. They thought that the Earth was shaped like a flat plate, and they were afraid to approach its edge so as not to fall into the abyss. For centuries, people also believed that the Earth was the unmoving center of the

Universe. People thought and considered reliable only the information that their eyes saw and their ears heard. The only reality for them was that what their senses could observe. In the 6th-7th centuries AD, people continued to live with incorrect beliefs. For example, they believed that a person could not fly through the air. For them this has been a reality for several centuries. If you take a closer look at all these examples, it will become even more obvious that humanity has always lived and lives today with erroneous ideas about almost everything. This refers to the "visible" and "invisible" worlds for the human eye. People have always felt and realized that the Universe and each "individual" are "controlled" by certain powerful invisible Forces. While suffering, people always wanted to receive help from them. To establish contact with them, they made gods from wood, stone or gold visible to their eyes. These gods were created in the image and likeness of people or animals and were considered true gods. People worshiped them and made sacrifices to appease them. They believed that by bringing them gifts, these gods, made with their own hands, would be more merciful to them. But True Reality has never depended and does not depend on how we perceive it and what we think about it. Reality has always been, is and will be the way it is, the way it created itself. Reality does not depend on our thoughts or our senses of its perception. I think Moses could not have said to his people: "Everything you see, hear and understand is wrong." They would not believe him. But he knew how to help them see, hear and understand Reality correctly. According to Moses, the eradication of evil from each individual and society as a whole was the first and most important step towards a correct understanding of Reality and the only way to help them to reach the "Promised Land" where there was "Honey and Milk". Moses performed many signs and wonders before their eyes, but could not help them see, hear, and understand correctly. All the signs and wonders were created by him in the "outer" world. The reason preventing people from changing, seems, to have been not in the external world, not in Moses, but within each person. Moses explained to people how to do this, but everyone had to understand and eliminate this reason themselves. Moses, loving his people and not hoping that they would be able to understand and fulfil his commandments, decided to bring them to the "Promised Land" at any costs. He decided that only fear and punishment could lead them to the "Promised Land":

"The judges must make a thorough investigation, and if the witness proves to be a liar, giving false testimony against his brother, then do to him as he intended to do to his brother. You must purge the evil from among you. The rest of the people will hear of this and be afraid, and never again will such an evil thing be done among you. Show no pity: life for life, eye for an eye, tooth for tooth, hand for hand, foot for foot." (Deuteron. 19:18-21).

These are just some quotes from the Laws of Moses. A man, who picked up a stick from the ground on the Holy Sabbath day of the week, was to be punished to death for breaking the law of Moses for the sake of edification to others. Moses hoped that the only way to eradicate evil from all society and from each person was through fear and punishment. He considered "evil" to be the main cause of people's misunderstanding, blindness and deafness. So, for the Israelis the image of God, thanks to the Laws of Moses, became twofold. God became for them, on the one hand, an avenger, punishing everyone for violating His (Moses) Laws, and on the other hand, a benefactor, abundantly blessing everyone, including descendants, for every right deed.

Jesus Christ was born in the cradle of the strict Laws of Moses. But despite this, he showed the world a completely different understanding of the character of God and the Divine Essence.

"Love your enemies, bless those who curse you, do good to those who hate you, and pray for those who persecute you" (Matt 5:44).

He wanted the same thing as Moses: to return man to his "original" state, to the "Kingdom of Heaven" or "Promised Land", here, on earth, and right now. As with Moses, one of the essential conditions was eradication evil from every person and society as a whole. The method was completely different: non-resistance to evil by violence.

"You have heard that it was said, Eye for eye, and a tooth for a tooth. But I tell you, do not resist an evil person. If someone strikes you on the right cheek, turn to him on the

other also. And if someone wants to sue you and take your tunic, let him have your cloak as well. If someone forces you to go one mile, go with him two miles. Give to the one who asks you, and do not turn away from the one who wants to borrow from you" (Mat 5:38-42).

The purpose of non-resistance to evil through violence, I think, is clear to everyone and is to stop the geometric progression of evil. Mutual revenge catastrophically increases anger and aggression in an individual, an entire nation, and a society of people. In geometric progression, evil and aggression over a minor incident often develop into hatred, hostility, bloodshed and war. Jesus Christ left specific commandments for his followers, following which a person can restore his true nature.

"Whoever has my commandments and obeys them, he is the one who loves me. He who loves me will be loved by my Father, and I too will love him and show myself to him" (John 14:21).

This phrase suggests that the main thing for people is not just to glorify Christ, but, most importantly, to fulfill His commandments. But, unfortunately, His commandments, like the commandments of Moses, turned out to be inaccessible to people's understanding to fulfill them. Throughout human history, people have grossly violated one of the most important commandments of Jesus Christ: not to resist evil with violence. Examples: wars with Muslims for the "Holy Sepulcher", centuries-old wars between Catholics and Protestants, Christians and Muslims, and so on. This is just a short list of "blindness", "misunderstanding" and failure to live according to the commandments of Jesus Christ. People have always wanted to escape the captivity of suffering, disease, poverty and dissatisfaction. They lived in the past and live now with hopes in the Higher Powers, believing that they exist and can help. It turned out that it is difficult for humanity to understand how to establish harmonious contact with the Higher Powers, which people call God. To people who would like to know how to be in harmony with God, Jesus Christ said:

"A new command I give you: love one another. As I have loved you, so you must love one another." (John 13:34)

Not only Jesus Christ speaks about the importance of love for each other. All other religious teachings of the world say the same thing. Does humanity keep this commandment of Jesus Christ? Not! Money, power, and material wealth have become the central values today. Jesus Christ's commandment *"love one another as I have loved you"* was forgotten. We have made material values basis of our lives. Because of this, we lose the most important thing given to us: Real Life, True Joy, and Grace. The "reasons" misleading humanity to understand Reality correctly are, it seems, an internal part of us. It distorts, refracts, and changes the strength and direction of the information sent to us from True Reality. Distorted perception makes us "blind, deaf, and not understandable. Phrases

"Until this day the Lord (God) has not given you a heart to understand, eyes to see and ears to hear" and

"This is why I speak to them in parables: Though seeing, they do not see, though hearing, they do not hear or understand"

said to people thousands of years ago, I think, are also relevant to all of us and right now.

Evil continues to live in humanity, preventing us from being kind and loving and make us live in suffer and dissatisfaction.

Science and Spirituality

Many generations have tried to find the roots of our blindness, deafness and misunderstanding and eradicate them from human society. With the development of scientific and technical knowledge, it has become somewhat easier to follow this path. In the past, there was only one Bible for the entire society. Once a year, all the people gathered in the Temple, listened to the reading of the Bible, received instructions, and studied them. Today, media and books are available to almost everyone. Science is penetrating deeper into the knowledge of the world. What previously seemed mystical, inexplicable and incomprehensible to our ancestors has become the norm for us. If we compare the knowledge that our distant ancestors possessed, say, at the time of Jesus Christ, and the capabilities of modern man, then we can say that this is "heaven and earth." We know (we think) much more. We have advanced in science, creating various devices, mechanisms and technologies. Our ancestors, for example, knew nothing about electricity. For them, out of their ignorance, it did not exist. But there was always electricity. The ether that people now use to propagate radio waves and transmit information has always existed. Telecommunications Information, and all other systems and technologies known to us today have always existed. But they were unknown to our ancestors and did not exist for them due to their ignorance. Scientific knowledge now gives us a concrete understanding of many phenomena and life processes. And some of the youths often have a question: why do we need spiritual knowledge when there is science? Yes, scientific knowledge reveals a lot to us. But relying on it as the basis of our lives, I think, is deeply mistaken. Science did not create Reality. The Earth, Sun, planets, sky, ether, gravity, magnetism and planetary systems are not the product of human hands or minds. Some other higher Intelligence created all this and placed humanity in the middle of it. For us there is no life outside this environment. True Reality and its Laws manifest themselves and live in and through all creation. The Supreme Invisible Intelligence, which we call God, determined, established the foundations of the Universe, its nutrition and wisely controls all its creation. Whether we understand it or not, this Supreme invisible Mind was and is everywhere and in everything. No matter how a person competes with this Mind, he will not be able to remake this Reality. He can partially find out how the Laws of the Universe work, and, knowing this, make a "scientific discovery". Science has not created, for example, Newton's law. Science can only "discover" what exists in True Reality. Any devices, mechanisms, and technologies "created" by a person are only the discovery of specific Laws existing in True Reality. "Discovery" allows people to use this knowledge to create devices and mechanisms that are convenient for us. If there were no ether through which radio waves travel, there would be no communication and information devices such as radio, television, etc. The True Reality created the ether and everything else for specific purposes in and for itself. Television, audio, video, all devices, computers, travel cards, bank cards, navigators, and everything else cannot work without the Communication Fields and Forces of the Universe that have always existed.

For some people, the desire to know, to penetrate the unknown, dominates over everything. Scientists, because of a great desire to "know," in 19th century discovered that the world consists from the smallest particles of atoms and molecules. For this discovery, scientists needed to create tools that helped them unconditionally believe in the existence of these particles. Now the whole world knows about the presence of atoms and molecules. But what is interesting is that the existence of these particles was known to the Great Spiritual Sages as early as 6000 years before our era. It mentioned in all ancient scriptures of the East (Upanishads, Bhagavad-Gita, etc.). They did not need any instruments for this knowledge. The prophets having renounced all other desires and interests, entering a state of enlightenment, successfully achieved their goal of knowing the Truth. Thus, these holy people realized the Supreme Reality, which lies beyond all forms and symbols. This sage's knowledge is one of the proofs that man is trying his best to create various systems and devices to understand the world around him better, whereas, on the contrary, all knowledge belongs and is in his internal system. Our achievements in science and technology are only a tiny part of the "discoveries" of how the unchanging and inexhaustible Universal Mind, God, who was, is, and will always be, governs the entire Universe. The most rational, in my opinion, is to link spiritual and scientific knowledge together to help us understand the existing World a little more correctly. True Reality has never depended on what we "think" about it or how we perceive it. Unfortunately, we do not pay enough attention to the invisible Laws of Life established for everyone by the Founder of the Universe. We don't delve deeply enough into their Essence. There's just no time. We must earn money and live as if we are "separated" from the existing True Reality that gives Life and fills everyone and everything with the Light of True Knowledge, Joy and Satisfaction. We do not obey these Laws and live according to our own rules, suitable only for us.

All devices, mechanisms, and technologies created by man are just toy's copies of the

Laws of the Universe. The Universe is like a "living computer." It nourishes, illuminates, records, reproduces, reads and stores all information about everything and everyone (and does not sell it to third parties). This program exists everywhere and in everything, in us, around us, and permeates all visible and invisible worlds. Without its presence, there is nothing. We cannot hide or isolate ourselves from its magnetic, gravitational, and all other forces and fields. Where could we hide from them? Even the grave won't help us doing it. In addition, there are thousands of undiscovered energy forces, such as life and love. We know about them from our sensations, but they have not yet been studied scientifically.

An unplugged computer, our best friend today, is just a piece of metal and plastic. It will not be able to provide us with information and communication services. The computer must not only be included in a single provider circuit, but also charged with energy, which can only be obtained with the help of energy generators that use the natural (God's) forces of the Universe such as the force of falling water, wind energy, solar energy, nuclear forces, and so on. A computer has all the necessary mechanisms to do its job, but even if it is connected to an Internet service provider and not charged with power, it is again a useless piece of metal. The same applies to the provider. It also needs to be charged with energy, which it can only receive from the energy sources of the Universe. An independent from the world person is like a computer disconnected from the network of the provider and the electricity supplier.

All man-made tools and devices are only striking examples of what is inherent in the very internal structure of man and the world around him (or us). We are an integral part of this huge and wise system through which, like an electric current, the power of life flows in all its manifestations. Marxism-Leninism introduced to the world the idea that "matter" is primary and consciousness is secondary. However, spiritual teachers say the opposite:

"Spirit is the Primordial Principle and the Parent of everything."

Everything we call "material substance" is created by Spirit. "Matter" is also "spiritual substance". Unlike the Eternal Spirit, "material substance" is not eternal and, after passing through certain cycles of development, returns to its original "Spirit". Everything that science has discovered and will discover in the future belongs to the Progenitor of Everything. He, God, is the Progenitor of man and the entire Universe. This is not only my opinion, but also the opinion of all great spiritual mentors: Jesus Christ, Buddha, Krishna, great Yogis and many, many others. It's hard to disagree with them, isn't it???

Who is my master?

Have you ever asked yourself this? Really, who is my master? Am I my master or not? So, who am I? Looking in the mirror, I see my height, skin color, eyes and hair. It's me. I can touch myself and run my hand through my hair and skin. I can even sniff and lick myself with my tongue. Based on this, I can say unequivocally: I am my body. My body is my master. However, sometimes we want to do something, but we feel a lack of strength. Without enough strength, we can't do anything at all, or, worse, we can't even get out of bed. No energy. Lack of energy deprives us of activity. Without enough energy, we cannot do what we want or need. We lie on the couch, eat or watch TV shows that we don't need or even like. So, our body depends not only on itself, but also on what gives it the strength and energy to desire, feel and fulfill these desires. We can call this energy whatever we want, but it is that what gives us the "life force" for desires and their fulfillment. We often neglect this invisible gift and waste this "Life Force" on trifles. But when we understand that "life" can leave the body, only when we realize its importance. Only then do we begin to "clearly" understand that what we often spend on trifles is our most priceless treasure. People are ready to work miracles, run, drink bitter herbs, give up their favorite cutlets and chops, and much more, in order to survive. If the "life force" leaves the body, then this body becomes motionless, cold, feels nothing, has no desires or thoughts and begins to decompose, turning back into the earth. There can be only one conclusion: the body is not our complete master. Our true master is the intellectual energy that contains the life force. This "elixir of life" exists within us in an invisible form.

Spiritual Masters call this energy Divine Spirit (or Holy Spirit). They say that this elixir of Life, Spirit, is the only existing indivisible, eternal Substance that gives life to everything.

Then who am I? Am I a body or something else? The Bible and other scriptures say that man is in the image and likeness of God. God is Spirit. According to the statements of all enlightened spiritual teachers, a person is not a body, but a Spirit living in a body. One day in the past a man identified himself as a separated from the world form and said: I am the body. It wasn't his name. Out of his ignorance, he "borrowed" another name for himself with characteristics alien to his nature. But you know, everything you borrowed will have to be paid back one day.

If the Spirit is our master, why is it so difficult to understand and acknowledge it? That's why, I think.

The Bible says that man, when God created the earth and heaven, had enormous spiritual power. He had to carry out and implement God's plans. The man successfully fulfilled his mission for a long time. God gave man the power to choose and give names to all whom the Lord God created. The free choice of man at that time was always the same as in God's plan.

«*Now the Lord God had formed out of the ground all the beasts of the field and all the birds of the air. He brought them to the man to see what he would name them; and whatever the man called each living creature, that was its name. So, the man gave names to all the livestock, the birds of the air and all the beasts of the field.*" (Genesis 2:19-20)

The name that man had to give to each creature was not a simple word that we usually use on a daily basis. It was the Living Word. A person had to fill a name, a word, with sound vibrations containing a mental program, plan, for the development and manifestation of each being. The word itself (or name) played the role of a ladle or form. It is impossible to carry water from one place to another without any utensils. It will spill. The same thing happens with words and names. Energy for its transmission in a vast space for its implementation must be poured into some form so that it does not splash out and dissolve in this space. This form was the word or name. Man had to pronounce a name for each creation, putting into the sound of this name all the energy that characterizes this name. For a long time, the man successfully coped with his functions. He was always in the presence of God, and God was always with him and in him. But one day, as the Holy Scripture says, a man violated the Law of God and ate the only fruit forbidden to him. Thus, he severed his relationship with God and with his Divine essence, and took a step away from the path that God had prepared for him. As a result, he saw himself as a separate bodily form and said to himself: "I am a body separated from everything and everyone, including God." The name "body" was not given to him by God. The man was prompted to give himself a new name by an erroneous new vision of himself. He saw himself as separated form from the rest of the world and gave himself the name "body". The characteristics of the new name were completely different from those that were originally included in him. By "borrowing" a new name he, thereby, endowed himself with new characteristics that were not characteristic of him. The mistaken name led him to a significant deviation in the perception of the True Reality. He began to see the world not with his spiritual essence, which is also the essence of the rest of the world, but with his physical eyes, which saw him as a body, separated from all other forms. He also began to see the world around him as separated forms from each other and from himself. The new name "body" must have impressed him so much that the person held it within himself, pondered, meditated, digested, rethought, and thereby increasingly endowed himself with qualities, properties and manifestations of his independence from the whole world, including God. After all, he had the power to give all earthly inhabitants a name corresponding to each of them. As a result, he also gave himself a new name "body" and began to live under a borrowed name. His real name "Spirit" ceased to receive sufficient spiritual nutrition and was gradually forgotten. And now, even if we understand that the name "Spirit" is more correct than "body," it has no place in our essence. We already have another name: body! This name, the body, has taken possession of our consciousness and turned inside into a huge, unshakable rock. This stone must be destroyed and split. But the name "body" is strong. It has grown so much that it occupies all the space inside and around us. Even attempts to change something of it seem impossible and useless, although Jesus Christ told us:*"You are the Sons of God."* But for us the name "body" has become as real as it was real for our distant ancestors that the shape of the Earth was a flat plate. If anyone at that time had told them that the Earth was not a flat plate, but had a completely different shape, that person would have been ridiculed or perhaps even killed. I think Jesus Christ wanted to show us that the whole world does not have separate, independent forms, but has always been and remains a single and indivisible spiritual body, which includes everything "material" and "spiritual".

"Do you not believe that I am in the Father and the Father is in me?" (John 14:10).

He showed us that it is not the body itself that is the basis of man, but the correctly oriented Spirit, the "Word of Life" in the body, that is his basis.

"Whoever wants to follow me, deny yourself, take up your cross and follow me." (Mark 8-34).

The words "deny yourself" unequivocally encourage and call us to part with the old outdated ideas about us as an independent body and, through an effort of will, to kill these obsolete ideas. They prevent us from developing in the right direction. Of course, this is not easy to do. However, all spiritual teachers of all nations, peoples, and religions say the same thing: deepening into the Truth gradually makes room for a correct understanding of the world and ourselves.

The origin and destiny of man

(According to the scriptures)

The Bible says: *"This is the account of the heaven and the earth when they were created. When the Lord God made the earth and the heavens - and no shrub of the field had yet appeared on the earth and no plant of the field had yet sprung up, for the Lord God had not sent rain on the earth and there was no man to work the ground..."* (Genesis 2: 4-5). So, *"The Lord God formed the man from the dust of the ground and breathed into his nostrils the breath of life, and the man became a living being"* (Genesis 2: 7).

According to the Holy Scriptures, the purpose of man was to cultivate the land. But what to cultivate? At the time when the Lord God created the earth and heaven *"no shrub of the field had yet appeared on the earth and no plant of the field had yet sprung up."* Everything had already been created, as the Bible says, but it was invisible to the human eye. It can be assumed that *"everything created"* existed on earth in the form of God's mental plans in forms of images for the planet. *"Everything created"* at that time was beyond human perception. The Lord God created man from the same earth on which He invisibly planted bushes and plants. Man, being "the earth", had to work with the same "earth" from which he was created. *"The Lord God breathed the breath of life into his nostrils, and man became a living being."*

God breathed the breath of life into the clay man and, thereby, connected the gross material earthly soil of the clay man with His subtle mental plans and ideas about the planet, not yet manifested in the gross material world. Man received through the breath of God all His plans, feelings, desires and thoughts. There was nothing else in the spirit of this man except the plans and ideas breathed into him by God. The plans and images of God were all that a person of that time had within himself. He knew nothing but God's plans. I think that the goal of man at that time was to work with not yet manifested images that existed in the mental plan of God for the earth and now existed in the consciousness of man. God entered into the clay-man, and the clay-man became the living God on earth. Man's task was to keep the images of God inside his body, which was the soil for planting God's "seeds", to love and store them in his heart and thoughts, where the Spirit of God, together with the spirit of the Man-God, filled them with life and gave them growth for visible manifestation on Earth. This time was the most significant time of cooperation between God and man. Man loved the ideas of God. Apart from them, he did not know anything else and did not have. He was God on earth, and God was always with him and in him. God's plans at that time were also the plans of man.

"Now the Lord God had planted a garden in the east, in Eden; and there He put the man he had formed. And the Lord God made all

kinds of trees grow out of the ground - trees that were pleasing to the eye and good for food. In the middle of the garden were the tree of life and the tree of the knowledge of good and evil". (Genesis 2 8-9).

"The Lord God took the man and put him in the Garden of Eden to work it and take care of it. And the Lord God commanded the man: "You are free to eat from any tree in the garden; but you must not eat from the tree of the knowledge of good and evil, for when you eat of it you will surely die." (Genesis 2, 15-17).

The Garden of Eden had an unlimited choice of trees with delicious and eye-pleasing fruits. A man was forbidden to eat the fruits only from one tree. The fruits of this tree were the only one temptation for man. God, being free in His desires, which were always good for everyone, gave Man the same freedom to choose desires (fruits from the trees or by the other words spiritual food). Man, indeed, was made in His image. Man, sacredly fulfilled the will of his Creator for an infinitely long time. But once he did something that was not in the program of his life. He suddenly desired to have a friend like himself, in his image and likeness. Among all the creatures of God, there was no one like him. Cooperating with God, man at that time possessed such great power that he was God on earth. I think this was his first mistake, which at that time was not too important, but one day it pushed him to a more serious one. So, God, who fulfills all man's desires, created from Adam's rib woman Eve. Eve was a part of Adam's body and, therefore, was the image and likeness of Adam. But Adam was the image and likeness of God. So, she was in the image and likeness of God as well. Part of Adam's power left him and went to Eve. Although they were in two different forms, they for a long time functioned as a single spiritual body. But over time, Eve became more and more distant from Adam. Since Adam was sometimes far from her and was busy with his own ideas and tasks, she began to experience the world not through him, as it was before, but through her Divine Essence or God. The spiritual connection between them became weaker. Two gods appeared on earth. Each of them had specific tasks, ideas and, as a result, different thoughts, desires and actions. God, creating Adam, breathed into him all His plans and spiritual power. This man was the only final image and likeness of God. After the division of Adam into two parts, God's power, His plans, and tasks partly remained in Adam but not equally passed to Eve. It made them both weaker. That is why they (Genesis 3:8-11) ate the forbidden fruit from the tree of the knowledge of good and evil. A weakened Spirit broke the energy balance in a man and woman and pushed them to wrong desires and actions. As a result, they broke the Law of Life and ate the forbidden fruit from the tree of the knowledge of good and evil. You know, food and drinks (alcohol, pesticides, etc.) can affect a person's perception of the environment, the work of the mind, internal vitality and the state of Spirit. When God asked: "*(Adam) where are you?*" Adam replied: *"I heard you in the garden, and I was afraid because I was naked; so, I hid."* (Gen 3:9-10}. Suddenly Adam saw himself hidden, separated from God as a naked body, and was frightened of violating His will. He no longer heard God's voice from within, but as if God was somewhere nearby. The Highest Divine World has the highest energy, frequency and density of wave vibrations. Lower energies have wider wave fluctuations and, therefore, cannot interact and change the Higher energy system.

They have neither the strength nor the ability to penetrate there. Only the highest Divine feelings and desires can exist, such as Eternal Love, Bliss, "Yes" and "Amen" in the Higher Spiritual World creating lightness, happiness and complete joy in souls and bodies. Feelings such as shame, fear, guilt and seeing oneself as a "separate from everyone" form have lower frequency vibrations compared to the Upper World. Such feelings cannot exist in the Divine World. Adam and Eve by birth belonged to the Higher World. Violating the rules of life weakened them spiritually and physically. Energy feelings and thoughts with low frequency vibration settled in them. Such feelings and thoughts previously had no right to even approach them. But they both retained them within themselves and, by their nature to give life to everything that was contained in them, developed and strengthened them. They could have gotten rid of them, but they didn't. This happened because the decrease in spiritual energy changed their perception of Reality. Trusting what their eyes saw, they began to identify themselves as forms separate from God and the entire World. Humanity, thus, descended from the Higher World of the energy level destined for them by fate to a lower one. Adam and Eve, I think, physically remaining in the same world where the Garden of Eden was created for them, "spiritually" moved abroad, to another country with lower energy. And now we, the descendants of Adam and Eve, are in a country to which we do not belong by birth and design, and we see the world distorted, as if through a darkened glass. If we try to increase our inner spiritual energy (this is not a very simple task, but with strong will and motivation it is still possible), then we can return to our world, to the Kingdom of Heaven, and right now.

The man and woman kept new feelings such as fear, guilt and independence from God and the World in their hearts and minds for a long unknown time, chewing and thinking about them. Gradually, a new image of themselves as a body became stronger in their minds. The Bible says that the word under certain conditions can become a flesh. And so, it happened. Being a flesh has become a reality for man as it was once a reality for our ancestors that the shape of the Earth was a flat plate. Man's Inner Essence, the cauldron of his life, was cut off from the world of his consciousness. Now we only vaguely guess, faintly feel the gracious touch of our Creator. God, once Real to man, now seems mystical and incomprehensible. And where is this God and his Spirit? After all, we are the "body." We live up to our name by satisfying primarily bodily needs and strengthening each other in this understanding. Superficial vision and awareness of oneself as a separate body is the root of all our problems, the progenitor of an excessive "ego", when everyone is on his own and is interested only in himself. I think the present goal of every person should be to find the way to our true parental home, where we are children and the image and likeness of our Heavenly Father. This is the path of our spiritual self-improvement.

The origin and destiny of man

(Philosophy, science, Holy Scripture)

Science, dividing the Earth into spheres, includes the biosphere as an integral part of the earth's spheres. Here is the simplest definition of the biosphere:

"The biosphere is a part of the earth's shell, which includes all living organisms, plants, animals, humans, unicellular organisms, and microorganisms. Living organisms live on the surface of the earth's crust and in its bowels, in the atmosphere and waters of rivers, seas, and oceans."

From this definition it follows that the biosphere is part of the earth's shell of a certain nature. The biosphere, through its vital activity, units the three spheres of the planet into one whole and influences the state of all of them. All spheres of the Earth also directly influence living organisms of the biosphere. I think, the biosphere can be considered as a spiritualized earth or living soil located between the dense deep "material" layers of the earth and its invisible subtle ether-like spheres in the atmosphere. A few words about the atmosphere.

You probably know that the upper layer of the atmosphere consists of the ionosphere, which, roughly speaking, surrounds the Earth like an eggshell and does not allow low-frequency wave vibrations to pass beyond its boundaries into the Universe. The scientific definition of the ionosphere states that the ionosphere is the part of the Earth's upper atmosphere ionized by solar radiation. It plays a vital role in atmospheric electricity and forms the inner edge of the magnetosphere. This has practical implications for humanity. Among other functions, it affects the propagation of radio signals to distant places on Earth due to their reflection. The ionosphere consists of many layers, different in their energy state. Each of the layers is so sensitive and intelligent that it is able to distinguish the smallest details of any low-frequency vibrations and, refracting them, direct them to the right place. Holy Scripture says nothing about the ionosphere. But there is something in the Bible that could explain the scientific definition of this phenomenon. The Bible says that the Holy Spirit recognizes our desires, feelings, and even the motives of our hearts and reflects them back in a magnified form to exactly where they came from. This role belongs to the ionosphere. So, this means that when someone does or wishes evil to someone else, the vibrations of those evil desires, sometimes after a long journey, sometimes very quickly, return intensified, exactly to the head of the one who sent them. Some people think that God was angry and punished them. But it's not right. This is the Spiritual Law established from the beginning of the world for everyone. The laws of life given to people by Holy people, in this case, were again scientifically confirmed. So, anyone who wants to do good for himself must live a Life according to the Laws of Life and respect them.

Let's return to the biosphere. All living organisms in the biosphere strive for existence, are aware of their existence, and want to enjoy it. They all have corresponding feelings and desires and manifest them through their body or flesh. The flesh of plants, animals, humans and all other forms of the biosphere is different, as is their nutrition. Since the principle of God's Life is the same throughout all creation, let us first look at the plant world, such as the grain or seed. In the first period of its development in the soil grain is fed primarily by the chemical elements and soil moisture of the earth and receives leading energy from the forces of the soil. Such nutrition causes specific changes in it. The grain softens, swells and bursts inside the ground. After these changes, the process of converting its contents into another form begins. The grain content is gradually transformed into the content of the "new creature". The structure and shape of the new creature is different from its parent. After some time, a new creation comes to the surface of the earth. The new world begins to intensively feed it with sunlight, gaseous substances, ether and additional moisture. At this stage, already rooted in the earth, it receives nourishment from the soil and the subtler spheres of atmospheric life; and the process of breathing begins in it. Plants, eating and inhaling more subtle energy food from the atmosphere, receive and acquire plant-appropriate feelings, desires and specific thoughts. The "new being" is aware of its existence and strives to enjoy it. The plant world is actually an intermediate layer of soil between the hard shell of the earth's soil and the more subtle components of Cosmic energy and is a continuation of the soil layer of its parent. By feeding on additional components of the atmosphere plants become more sensitive to receiving more subtle informative vibrations from the Universe and a more complete awareness of their existence. The process of grain transition to a higher structural form is accompanied by specific processes both in the grain itself and in the space surrounding it. This process, or we can say the Law, is the release of latent energy in the seed and the Universal program. The hidden power in the grain does not manifest itself until certain conditions arise for its manifestation. The computer program starts working if all cells are marked correctly. The same goes for grains or seeds. The transformation from one form to another begins if all the necessary conditions are met. These conditions are soil, heat and water. The grain, under the influence of earth, moisture, and heat softens, bursts and then begins to give all its contents to a new creation. A tiny sprout breaking through the ground is so fragile and delicate that it is simply amazing how it was able to break through the hard shell of the grain, and then the thickness of the earth. The energy forces released from the grain and the Universe directly contribute, I think, to this process. A weak sprout attracts the forces of the Universe and, thanks to the program inherent in everything, finds itself enveloped in a spacesuit of invisible vital forces. They protect and give him the strength to build and transform the structure of his body to a higher level and overcome obstacles. This energy guides a weak sprout through the hard layers of the earth, protects and surrounds it with attention and love. In my opinion, protecting the life of a newborn is one of the Laws of the Universe. This Law applies not only to the plant world, but to all manifestations of life. When the people of Israel fled from Egypt and were considered the "seed" of God, this Force of life was the very cloud that illuminated their path of escape from slavery and that one which blinded the eyes of their pursuing enemies. Plants and their bodies are essentially plant living soil. It is food for herbivores and humans. Man also eats meat, but only herbivores. Carnivorous animals mainly feed on herbivores. Plants, in fact, are food for both humans and animals, including predators. One famous proverb says: "The body is what we eat". Thus, it can be said, that the bodies of man and animals consist of plants and represent animated plant soil with more subtle sense organs. This increases their vitality and strengthens the internal structure of their bodies, turning this group into a kind of animated layer of soil, endowed with special abilities. Man and the main group of animals live on the surface of the earth. In addition to plant food, they also receive additional nutrition from gaseous elements of the atmosphere, sunlight, ether, moisture, as well as more intense exposure to electromagnetic, gravitational and other fields of the Earth and the Universe. A person, whose body consists of more "developed" living soil of the plant world, inhales atmospheric air in which the ideas and programs of the Creator of the Universe and those that, he created himself, live. These ideas or programs in the form of ether and even more subtle components of the Cosmic Living Mind nourish the human spirit, making a person more sensitive to the perception of subtle information vibrations of the Universe. Such nutritious food increases the ability of animals and people to become more aware of their existence and gives them unlimited opportunity to have desires, feelings and thoughts and to perform all the necessary actions for their implementation. Plant foods saturate a person not only with chemicals. This food contains living microorganisms necessary for the proper functioning of the human internal system. This is why eating raw plant foods is beneficial. Living microorganisms in processed foods are killed. People, inhaling air saturated with vitality and chemical elements, are exposed to the Sun, electromagnetic and gravitational radiation and through all this connect with the subtle Divine World. Thus, this group of organisms actually manifests itself as a layer of soil for sowing certain seeds, such as ideas, "words", desires and images. Human bodies are a layer of soil in which the Divine Mind lives. Thus, they connect the entire biosphere with the subtle Divine World of the Universe and have the ability to transform the "invisible", such as ideas, words, images and desires into the visible and vice versa. Such a program inside a person gives him, and therefore, to all of us, the freedom to choose from all the ideas and desires we need or like. Man is, in fact, the soil for sowing and cultivating ideas, desires, feelings, images and "words". The sower chooses and "sows" what he has chosen and expects to receive fruits from them. Everyone knows the law: "What you sow is what you reap." If we sow wheat, there will be a harvest of wheat. The person does not know all the processes occurring inside the earth and grain. But he is waiting for shoots. Every day he checks that everything is in order, removes weeds, waters and waits for fruit. Taking "material" food inside, a person also does not know what is happening inside his body. We do not know all those truly magical transformations and the enormous work that is invisibly carried out inside our body to process, assimilate and deliver absorbed nutrients to every cell and every organ of our body. But the spiritual-intellectual body within us has absolute knowledge of everything it needs to do for the best functioning of the entire organism at any given moment. He tells every organ, gland and cell what to do at every moment of our lives. All organs, cells and glands obey these commands and carry them out unquestioningly. Even if we did or ate something wrong, the spiritual-intellectual organism can independently and immediately make the best decision and resolve the situation in the best possible way. The same principle operates in the spiritual world of words, desires, thoughts and feelings. Every thought, word, desire or emotion can be considered as a grain of wheat planted in the soil of the human body. An idea or a desire must be constantly kept in the body, like a seed in the soil. One must by an effort of will keep this seed inside and take care that it not be eaten and destroyed by the weeds of other thoughts and desires. By consciously observing inner growth a person, thereby, warm it with the warmth and love of his "divine" soul. Then the one can expect the fruits of what he has sown within himself. We do not know how a thought or a word is transformed from an "invisible" form of an idea into a "corporeal" form, but just as one seed brings forth many times multiplied fruits, so the word we sowed into the soil of our soul gives its fruits multiplied many times over. Here is the parable of Jesus Christ about the seed and the Kingdom of God:

"This is what the Kingdom of God is like. A man scatters seeds on the ground. Night and day, whether he sleeps or gets up, the seed sprouts and grows, though he does not know it. All by itself, the soil produces corn - first the stalk, then the ear, then the full grain in the ear. As soon as the grain is ripe, he puts a sickle to it, because the harvest has come" (Mark 4: 26-29).

The words we speak and the thoughts we keep inside are very important. A person has power over them and can, at will, choose and change the wrong into a more correct one. This is what Moses told to his people about the importance of the "Word" we choose.

"Now what I am commanding you today is not too difficult for you or beyond your reach. It is not up in heaven so that you have to ask: "Who would ascend into heaven to get it and proclaim it to us so that we may obey it?" Nor is it beyond the sea so that you have to ask, "Who will cross the sea to get it and proclaim it to us so that we may obey it?" No, the word is very near you; it is in your mouth and your heart so that you may obey it. See, I set before you life and prosperity, death and destruction." (Deuteronomy 30: 11-15).

"This day I have set before you life and death, blessing and curses. Now choose life, so that you and your children may live." (Deuteronomy 30:19).

Jesus Christ said: *"From the days of John the Baptist until now, the kingdom of heaven has been forcefully advancing, and forceful men lay hold of it."* (Matthew 11:12).

It sounds simple, but it's not that easy to do. Lack of vital energy prevents most of us from taking control of our desires and thoughts. The fate and tasks of a person are different for those who lack vital energy and those who have reached the highest stage of spiritual development. The first are those who left the Kingdom of God's Light and entered the world of darkness. The goal of the vast majority is to overcome old thinking, gain correct understanding and find the path to their true parental home, to the Kingdom of God, to switch "material" egoistic thoughts, ideas, desires and words to higher ones, which are good both for the entire Universe and for each of us. The radio, a toy replica of what is built into the human internal system, operates with different types of waves. We must also be able to do this many times more perfectly. We must be able and can switch thoughts from one type of wave to another, just as a radio switches according to our choice to the programs we need. The main task of man on earth and what he came here for is to abandon the name "body" borrowed by man and return to himself the true name "Spirit" with all its corresponding characteristics. This is, as I think, the path of self-improvement and the main goal that we must achieve in this life. Well, avatars, I can only say one thing about them: they have become a source of vital energy and relevant knowledge for those who are in darkness. They, like the sun, shine into the world of darkness, giving us vital energy to see, hear and understand the world correctly.

The Visible and Invisible Worlds

(Differences and Similarity)

Most of us know that the invisible world exists, but we mainly know it with our minds, not with our hearts and consciousness. The visible world, which seems infinitely large to us, is only a small part of the invisible one. We are not always aware of the existence of the invisible world. But if you move down the keyboard of a musical instrument towards the bass, you will find that the sounds gradually become weaker and weaker. At some point we stop hearing them altogether. It may seem that sounds no longer exist. But they exist beyond our auditory perception. The difference between audible and inaudible sounds lies in the difference in their wave frequency oscillations. In fact, there are no barriers or boundaries between the visible and invisible world. One gradually turns into another. Everything visible and invisible is one indivisible whole. With the help of a sound amplifier we can hear sounds that we cannot hear with our ears. This proves that the world hidden from our perception exists and is just as real as the visible one. The visible world is just a continuation and expansion of the invisible world. All the differences between them lie in their distances from the energy source. Closer to the source, the energy is higher and the density of the form is lower. In the place closest to the source, everything "burns" with vital energy. The forms there can be, it seems to me, ideas, images, symbols and words. The further away from the energy source, the weaker the light energy and, as a result, the forms have a higher density. The nature and principles inherent in both, the visible and invisible world, should be the same for the entire Universe. This means that the mental image and the material form are of the same nature. The differences between them are in their energy forces and the densities of forms or state of their matters. Eastern spiritual teachers talk about five states of the manifested material world. They are: solid, liquid, fiery, gaseous and ethereal. Based on this, we can assume that the matter of the ethereal state is feelings, words, mental images and symbols. The nature of all states is the energy of mental light that gives life to everything. Mental images are closer to the source of energy and just as real as those "physical" forms that we often take as the basis of our lives. Under certain conditions, mental images can interact and energetically penetrate the "physical" body, causing appropriate changes in it.

Meditation and mind training can help us realize that the invisible world is real and we are all part of it. Interest and conscious attention to any subject, be it gross matter, a word or an idea, can attract the necessary knowledge from the Universe. Our interest, attention, feelings, desires, thoughts and actions are a continuation and expansion of our "I am". In other words, a person is as "big" as "big" his interest and attention to the world. A person's "size" includes his desires, feelings, thoughts, and actions. They form an integral part of our 'I am' and are the 'I am'. Interest and attention to the world makes a person limited or unlimited depending on his conscious interest and awareness. If we limit ourselves only to the material world and are aware of ourselves as "a body", we will be only that. One day, if we sincerely want it, we will be able to realize that we are limitless. Interest in knowing the Truth can make us Godlike. A deep interest in the True understanding of the world expands and deepens our understanding of ourselves to the limits of this interest. The words of the Great Buddha *"The Thousand-Armed Buddha grows into a giant reaching to the skies"* are an example of his spiritual understanding of himself and His Spiritual unity with the True Essence of God. Jesus Christ is also one example of such self-understanding. He said: *"Before Abraham was, I Am"* (John 8:58). I think he realized and understood himself as always existing from the very foundation of the world. He realized and "knew" himself not as a small body, "flesh", but as a part of the indivisible, eternal Divine Essence. He knew that he is an integral part of this Divine Essence, which has in Itself an invaluable unlimited reservoir of any absolute: knowledge, power, love, joy and fulfillment of all desires. A person tries to create various devices in order to better understand the world, while absolute knowledge about everything is stored inside him and belongs to him, built into his internal system. Jesus Christ told us: "*Seek first His Kingdom and His righteousness, and all these things will be given to you*" (Mathew 6:33). He did not order us first of all to seek material goods, to create various devices for the convenience of our lives, and then to seek the Kingdom of God. His words tell us otherwise. If we seek the Kingdom of God "within and around us", then what we need will be given to us from the invisible without much difficulty. The age-old inertia of thinking, negative experience, and lack of vitality - that is why it is so difficult to do this today. It is almost impossible for majority today not to identify ourselves with the name "body." The structure of the whole society keeps all of humanity in a small "material world" where people can only identify themselves as bodies. But the problem is that the body, the "flesh," is only a temporary home for invisible life energy. The body must completely obey this energy. Possessing the spiritual power to bring their ideas into reality people have managed to limit their real spiritual "I am" to the framework of the flesh, the same time disconnecting the spiritual "I am" from their consciousness and attention. On the other hand, excessive attention and unreasonable demands on the body have compacted it and created significant resistance to the energetic forces of the Universe. Extreme egoism, dependence only on bodily desires prevents the free influx of the finest light energy that carries life force into the inner body of a person. If one of two parallel resistances in an electrical circuit has a high resistance and the other has a low one, then more current will flow through the low resistance. A small amount of current will flow through a high resistance. The flow Energy of Life encountering a body with high resistance in the human consciousness on its way is weak. As a result, a person perceives distorted information. The invisible spiritual world is not only alive and existing but is also the foundation on which we must build the house of our life. Forces and Laws of the invisible Spirit created and "gave birth" to the earth, sky, sun, planets and everything in them. Spiritual sages say that practice is necessary to realize our inseparability from the boundless Spiritual world. The Scriptural promise is that those who seek knowledge will find it. Our desires and interests attract relevant knowledge from God's invisible reservoir of the Universe. Divine life force is everywhere: in our organs, body, spine, heart, circulatory system and every cell. We are in Him and He is in us. He, unclaimed, sleeps within us until we call upon Him, awaken Him and give Him all our attention.

"Call to Me and I will answer you and tell you great and unsearchable things you do not know" (Jer33: 3)

Moses told his people they did not need to travel far beyond the seas and high into the sky to find the Divine Essence. The body of the Spirit of God fills all living and inanimate existing forms and is the inner Essence of each of us. To achieve awareness of oneself as an integral part of the Divine Essence is not easy and depends on the inner spiritual state of each person. Internal factors include karma, willpower, desires, thoughts, etc. Like a seed planted in the soil, the idea of a person, sown in his soul, develops and gains strength. No one, including the one who sows it, knows how long it will take to receive "spiritual fruit". But once sown into the soul it remains in the subtle body of a person in the form of energy information. Having such an idea or "seed" within us, we will not find ourselves in the position of an ass, which, as Jesus Christ said: *"...walked 100 miles around the millstone. When they untied him, he was still in the same place".* Having lived many lives (reincarnations) without such an idea, a person does not develop spiritually, or his development is weak. Jesus Christ said:

"Do not store up for yourselves treasures on earth, where moth and rust destroy, and where thieves break in and steal. But store up for yourselves treasures in heaven, where moth and rust do not destroy, and where thieves do not break in and steal. For where your treasure is, there your heart will be also" (Matt 6: 19-21).

All the information, words, ideas, feelings, thoughts, images and secret impulses of our heart, recorded in the past and present, are active and alive in us. They determine our destiny. Our soul is *"a place where neither moth nor rust can penetrate and destroy it* (except ourselves), *and where thieves cannot penetrate and steal."*

Souls live after our physical death and carry on all the "baggage" of information we recorded in them. Let's take another look at the visible to us world to understand better how invisible one works.

If you plant a grain that has lain in a dry, warm place for 5-7 years, water it, and the sun's rays warm it, it will begin to grow. His internal growth program did not disappear for 5-7 years. The grain patiently waits for special conditions under which it can fulfill its main task - reproduction of the species. The laws of life are the same for all creatures of the visible and invisible worlds. The grain transforms its content into a new form under special "material" conditions. Our souls, like grains, also await special demands. These requirements are spiritual. It is we, ourselves, who must spiritually create these conditions sowing the desired "idea (or seed)" into the soil of our soul, nourishing and watering it with love and attention. We can only do this spiritually. Only spirit can unite everything into one whole. We can become one with all of creation through the energy of life and love that fills our bodies and everything around us. This cannot be done by material bodies. But we, assigning the leading role to the body, are trying to connect with the entire Universal system through the body. Thus, we aggravate our condition, turn everything upside down, loading the "body" with overwhelming tasks, exhausting and weakening it, gradually destroying the house in which our soul lives. If the "house" becomes uninhabitable, the "owner", Spirit, leaves it. But after the so-called "death", when the "owner" leaves the house, our souls continue to live, retaining all the information accumulated over all our previous lives. After a rest the soul builds a new home for itself, a new body that appears in the world with all the karmic information inherited from previous existences. Without a "master" the body "dies" and decomposes. The body, I think, can be seen to some extent as an eggshell. The eggshell holds the white and yolk until they turn into a chicken. The white and yolk will spread without a shell, and the chicken will not be born. The soul in this "material" world cannot develop and bear fruit if it is not in the body, like white and yolk in an eggshell. The body isolates the inner content of a man from the energy space with a lower vibration frequency than his soul. Without the body, its inner energy content would dissolve and disappear. The soul, after rest, creates a new home, a new body. And all processes begin anew. To turn its content into a new creation a person must put all his spiritual content into it, leaving only an empty bodily shell in which it spent a certain time of its development. If you have ever sowed seeds, then I think you could not fail to notice how a new sprout growing out of the ground retains on its head the empty shell of the seed from which it grew. The seed must burst and thereby open the door for a new creation to emerge from it. The new creation is essentially the same seed turned into a stronger plant capable of multiplying that tiny seed many times over. The shell of the grain must necessarily burst so that its contents can be transformed into a new form. The same thing happens with the body. It must be torn apart (we say it must die) in order for all its spiritual content to be turned into new "spiritual" creation. If you have ever planted potatoes, you know that on some bushes only pieces of the peel remain in the ground from the mother potato. In this case, the potato gave up its entire body for growth. There we reap a rich harvest. But in some places the potatoes remain intact, only slightly dented and dried out. The harvest there is poor. This shriveled potato "didn't think" to take care of its reproduction to continue to live in its offspring. Perhaps it was "thinking" about how best to decorate the surrounding land, buy good furniture, make life more comfortable, and didn't have a correct understanding of its main goal. The same thing, I think, happens to us. To become a new "spiritual" being, a person must give all his spiritual (and material, which is also a product of the spirit) contents. When the body can no longer hold the growing fetus inside, it must release it and the body must be torn apart. A woman gives life to her biological children and does not die. This happens, I think, because she is of a spiritual nature, and not carnal. She, like all mankind, descended from her highest spiritual level to the level of animals and even lower. The primary task of any person on earth is not to give birth to biological children (although this is also very important in our position), but to give life to a spiritual fetus. Only in this case do we say that the person dies. The body is torn apart and only then can the invisible spiritual being come out of its "eggshell" and embark on a new path of development. We say: "The man has died." But this is only that the "fruit" came out of the shell, in which it got stronger and developed to a certain state.

The "spiritual child," when he becomes large and strong, leaves his cramped place where he underwent special development; and moves on to another, new colossal world, which he has to learn and go through. The body, like an eggshell, "dies." But our soul, our true essence, is alive. The soul, leaving the body, retains all the information accumulated in the past and present life. Having rested, she builds a new home, appearing in a new body with all the karmic information inherited from previous lives, or continues to develop further along the path prepared for it in the higher spiritual world, no longer returning to the gross material world. In order not to return to earth again, in the world of suffering and pain, a person must produce spiritual fruit. Then Father and son will be One. This is the highest purpose of man on earth. Jesus Christ said: *"Know the truth and the truth will set you free."* What to be free from in order to be free? The answer is simple: from slavery to serving a false worldview, from slavish fulfillment of all the harmful, desperate commands of our exhausted, sick body. Truth restores strength and health of spirit and body. Knowing the "Truth" makes a person, as I understand, so powerful that he gains the ability to resurrect dead bodies to life. In the event of a voluntary renunciation of life or an accident, such a person will be able, I think, to return his body to life within three days. The material world in which we live is transitory. The Soul is eternal. "Choose life to live," said Moses. Everyone wants to choose life. This choice is good for us. But it takes efforts and is not easy to do. But as they say: with God all things are possible!

The Essence of the Universe

There are many scientific theories, hypotheses, philosophical reflections, folklore and religious teachings about the origin and essence of the Universe. We must not ignore the idea that God, the First Cause of all energies, powers, life, and knowledge created the world. He, the energy powers of Live, Love, Joy, Yes and Amen, is in everything. Throughout a history, all people of different faiths and cultures have believed and continue to believe in God. Even the most notorious atheists, in moments of hopelessness, suddenly remember and understand that there must be a final Higher Authority, a Power that can help and to which they can turn for help even at the very last and fatal moment of life. This Higher Power is God. In ancient Greek philosophy, the name of this Essence was Logos. "Logos" was considered the World Mind, the Law and the Ruler of the world, determining everything that happens. Their idea was that Logos would periodically light up and then go out. During the outbreak, the world arises from this Fire and returns to it when it goes out. Eastern spiritual and religious teachers say the same things about God: He is Mind, Law, Thought, Fire and Light. They also include in it the word "God" and Man as an inseparable part of the Essence of God. The Christian Bible says the same thing:

"In the beginning was the Word, and the Word was with God, and the Word was God. He was with God in the beginning, through him, all things were made; without him, nothing was made that has been made. In him was life, and that life was the light of men. The light shines, but the darkness has not understood it" (John 1:1-5).

John expanded the ancient Greek understanding of "Logos" or "God." He included in the concept of God *"the word that God had"* and that *"The word was "God."* Man, according to John, was included in the concepts of the Word, God, the word God, Essence of God, Light, and Life. God-like yogi Swami Sri Yukteswar Giri in his book "Holy Science," describes 14 areas of the Divine Essence in the Universe. The seven stretches from the Eternal Essence of the Universe to the gross material world. The human body is a miniature copy of the Universe. So, there are the same seven realms in it. *"The human body is built in the image of our Universe. Therefore, if a person directs his attention to his inner "I" and practices this persistently and diligently, he will see the Spiritual Light in these centres"* (The Seven Chakras), yogi Swami Sri Yukteswar Giri says.

Let me briefly describe the spheres of the Universe and man given by him. In the Bible, these spheres are called heavens (4th heaven, 5th heaven, and so on).

A) The central supreme kingdom of God (seventh kingdom). This is the only True Essence of the entire Universe. None of the creatures of Darkness or Light can give it any definition. Therefore, the seventh central sphere is called "Nameless". (For Christians this is seventh heaven).

B) Sphere of the Holy Spirit (sixth sphere). This sphere represents Eternal Patience, for the peace of this sphere cannot be disturbed by any limited idea. Even the Sons of God cannot know this kingdom. That's why it's called "Unavailable".

C) Sphere of Spiritual Transformation (fifth sphere). This is the Kingdom of Spiritual Light, the Sphere of the Sons of God. In this area the idea of separate existence is born. This area is beyond her understanding of the dark-spawn. It's called "Incomprehensible".

D) Sphere of the Atom (fourth sphere). This is the sphere of the beginning of the creation of darkness, from which the Spirit is reflected. This is the connecting link between the spiritual and material world. This is the "Tenth Door," or, as Christians say, "Pass through the Cross."

E) The sphere of magnetic and electrical aura of the manifestation of the Atom (third sphere). There are no creations, sense organs or objects. This is the "Great Vacuum".

G) The sphere of electrical properties of the atom (second sphere). There is no gross matter here, only subtle properties are represented. This is "Normal Vacuum".

H) The sphere of gross matter of forms is the "first and lowest sphere." This area is perceived by everyone and at any time.

Swami Sri Yukteswar Giri told us: *"Consequently, if the human body is in the image of our Universe, a person must direct his attention to his inner "I." One who practices this persistently and diligently will see the Spiritual Light in these centres"* (Seven Chakras).

Following the above description, the Spiritual Light manifests in the third Sphere and represents the Kingdom of the Sons of God. We cannot see this Light. But this Light was, is and will always be in us and in everything that exists in the entire Universe. For to gain some knowledge about Spiritual Light, we can try to gain some understanding of sunlight, which is a part of Spiritual Light.

Sunlight has long occupied the minds of scientists. All types of light, including solar light, are composites and derivatives of

Spiritual Light and have similar characteristics. One of the main characteristics of sunlight is that all creatures love the sun and its warmth. Its rays fill everything and everyone with joy and inner satisfaction. How is the nature of sunlight different from material forms or "bodies"? According to science, all material forms are composed of atoms assembled into molecules. Each atom is made up of negatively charged particles called electrons, as well as a nucleus. The nucleus consists of neutrons, which have no electrical charge, and positively charged protons. Electrons orbit around the nucleus. Like all light sources, sunlight is radiant energy and has a wave nature. Its rays are called photons. Waves of sunlight travel through space at the fastest speed known in the Universe: 300,000 kilometres per second. A photon manifests itself not only as a wave, but also as a particle, a segment of an electromagnetic wave. This segment is called a quantum. Waves of different types of light differ from each other energetically. Their energy depends on their wavelength. The longer the wavelength, the lower its energy. Our eyes perceive light only in a certain range of wavelengths. Visible light for us is the sun and electric lamps. Gamma rays, X-rays, and ultraviolet rays are also light, but their particles have very high energy and wavelengths too short to be seen by our eyes. For the same reason, we cannot see the rays of Light from the Primary Source, from God. The body of the Sun, according to scientific concepts, is not a solid body like the Earth. The surface temperature of the Sun reaches 6000°C. At such high temperatures, any metal or stone turns into gas. So, according to scientific data, the Sun consists of gases: 75% hydrogen and 25% helium. In the past, scientists believed that sunlight and heat were the result of combustion. But the surface of the Sun has been hot for hundreds of millions of years, and during this long period, the body of the Sun would have to burn out. Some scientists believe that the sun generates heat through processes similar to those that occur in an atomic bomb. Here is one of the theories that I liked the most.

Due to the enormous temperature, tiny particles of gases that form the body of the Sun fly at a very high speed colliding with each other with a great force. From such collisions all the electrons "exfoliate" from the atoms. Therefore, all particles in the sun are "naked." The Sun has "bare" atomic nuclei and "bare" electrons. The nucleus of an atom consists of positively charged protons and neutrally charged neutrons. Protons with the same positive charge, colliding with each other, would bounce off each other and fly apart in different directions. But inside the nucleus powerful forces firmly bind neutrons and protons. They are so strong that when nuclei collide, instead of bouncing off, they press the nuclei tightly against each other and combine them into one, despite the presence of equally charged protons in them. From this we can assume and note how good it is to be in a neutral position, which is extremely strongly associated with everything positive, as between neutrons and protons. Atoms of different substances differ in the number of protons and neutrons in the nucleus itself. For example, If you add 1 proton and 1 neutron to the nitrogen nucleus, the result will be the nucleus of a completely different atom. It will be oxygen. According to this theory the Sun's body contains hydrogen and helium gases. Hydrogen is one of the lightest substances known in the world. Its nucleus consists of only one proton and one neutron. Helium is also from light one. There are only two protons and two neutrons in the nucleus. Iron, for example, has fifty-six protons and neutrons in its nucleus, while gold has two hundred and ninety-seven! Scientists suggest that after "wandering" at high speed, so to speak, the hydrogen nuclei are combined. When they stick together, they form a helium nucleus + two to three photons (a particle of light) and other small particles. Many such mergers are happening at the same time. All photons generated this way are scattered in all directions, including toward the Earth. The sun converts hydrogen into helium to form photons. It's only my guess that there should be a reverse process for converting helium into hydrogen. This theory is only a hypothesis and is suitable, I think, only for the atomic-molecular understanding of things. But the question arises about such an inexhaustible force of protons and neutrons cohesion in the nucleus. Where does it come from? What is the source of these forces from? Why don't the gaseous elements that make up the solar globe dissipate in the vacuum surrounding the Sun? What is that that keeps them in the shape of a ball? For many, this is just a mystery. But this is the fact and is an existing reality. These forces exist in real life. Sages and some scientists are sure of the existence of a fiery Light (Logos or God), which determines and rules the world, endowing it with His mentally created "best" ideas, containing a unique, unchanging, and infallible program for the preservation, development, and manifestation of everything that exists. The above mentioned theory shows that the Sun, as a fireball consisting of gaseous elements, is not a light source. The source of light is an invisible force hidden within it. The program of this source controls all the processes occurring in it. We do not know much about God's light. We can't see this light. We also don't know much enough about sunlight yet. We know, for example, only that "white sunlight" is a mixture of photons with different wavelengths. If a glass prism were placed in the path of a sunbeam, the "white sunlight" would separate into seven colours with different wavelengths. Some knowledge of sunlight can help us understand and characterize the nature of the Light of the Primal Source. A prism placed in the path of a sunbeam refracts and decomposes the white light of the sun's rays, depending on their energy level, into seven colours: red, orange, yellow, green, blue, dark blue, and violet. Red light photons have the lowest energy and are the least deflected by a prism. Violet photons have the highest power, so the deviation is more significant than the rest. The rest of the colours ranges energetically from red to purple. Knowing this, we can conclude that our selfish, low-frequency desires and thoughts more easily penetrate our consciousness and easily take root in us. The ideas of God have the greatest vital energy and therefore are refracted in our consciousness most strongly, changing their strength and direction. Hence our blindness, deafness, and misunderstanding of the nature of things and difficulties with their perception. If you put another prism in the path of the rays of the resulting rainbow, then you can again collect them into one white beam. The sun's rays, focused by a lens on one point, create such a great force at that point that fire arises there. With the help of a lens, you can do wood burning on the most ordinary, not too-sunny day. I think this is one of the essential characteristics that we should keep in mind. Light rays concentrated at one point become so powerful that they create a fire. According to the ancient Greek understanding Logos is the fire from which the whole world comes out. Divine Fire, I think, is the mental ideas of the Higher Powers, concentrated at one point, where its power is so great that it "draws or creates" this World from this "fiery" point. And this fiery point is not some kind of fiction, but a real fact , true reality.

There are several interesting facts about photons. They have enormous potential energy without having an electromagnetic charge (at rest), while quanta, the particles of a light beam, have no mass (at rest). An uncharged and massless (seemingly non-existent to us) particle of light has unlimited potential power. What we also know about photons is that they can interact with denser objects and, at a certain intensity of light, be absorbed by atoms and molecules of that substance. Dense objects, "feeding" on the energy of photons, become more charged and, therefore, more energetically viable. It is "Divine God's Alchemy". It is carried out not only in the world of breath and "living" forms. Interesting visual transformations can be seen everywhere and in everything in nature.

Let's take minerals as an example. Coal and diamond. What do they have in common? It seems nothing. But they both consist of the same chemical element - carbon. Coal turns into diamond in the depths of the earth under high pressure and temperature. Since denser substances are able to absorb sunlight, it can be assumed that Spiritual Light has the same qualities and gives everything even more energy for "Divine Alchemy" than sunlight. In a "live or die" situation, some of the coal under pressure and high temperatures chose to "live!" instead of dying. Finding no other way to salvation, they turned to the Higher Powers for help. Even the most notorious atheists know: God is the last chance for salvation in moments in life when you have to choose "live or die." *"If you ask, it will be given to you,"* says the Bible. This is one of God's promises. Everyone wants to "live" and enjoy life, but not everyone has the willpower and perseverance to make the leap from death to life. Only a tiny fraction of coal has managed to give up all other desires except one: "to live." Directing, as I think, all feelings (all types of forms have them) not to the outside world, but to the center of themselves, they asked the Higher Powers for life and affirmed it within themselves. And it was heard and given to them. Spiritual Light contains Life Force and fills everything with Life. This became their mantra, prayer, and a primary spiritual food. Life energy was "eaten" and absorbed by them. By eating "real food," the coal received enough vitality to go through all the miraculous transformations from its mortal state into an immortal diamond. Such "Spiritual God's Alchemy" performs by Spiritual Light only. The difference between the two minerals lies in the structure of the atomic bonds and the percentage of impurities. Diamond is pure carbon. It contains practically no impurities (less than 0.1%). Coal is the same carbon, but with an admixture of other substances, approximately 15-25%. Differences in the properties of coal and diamond are associated with the presence and percentage of impurities of other substances in them and the difference in their crystal lattice structure. Diamond has the strongest crystalline atomic structure. Light easily penetrates it and, intensifying, reflecting and refracting in it, makes it the source of this Light. Among all known materials, diamonds have the highest hardness, compressive strength, crack resistance, chemical resistance and inertness to aggressive environments, and are also the simplest in chemical composition. A diamond here on Earth has transformed its body from the state of "mortal coal" into the body of an "immortal" crystalline diamond. There is one more point to which I would like to draw your attention. The diamond's rhombic facet is very strong at the corners, but a little weaker in the middle. The corners of its facets, like the mythical Atlantes, support the main strength of the diamond's body on their shoulders. Knowing this helped me understand the words of Jesus Christ: *"The stone the builders rejected has become the capstone"* (Mat. 21-42).

In mineralogy, there are many examples of the transformation of minerals from simple to crystalline forms. Man is also able to absorb sun's and Divine Light and be saturated with them. Remember how suddenly a sense of joy arises when the sun appears on a cloudy rainy day? The sun, its energy, penetrating everything, produces many reactions and transformations in the "physical" body, giving an impulse of power to the nervous system that directly connected with all systems of both gross matters and the subtlest ether bodies within a man. But sunlight is only one of the components of the Light of the Creator.

The Energy of the Creator's Light must be much more significant and be proper spiritual food for everyone. This "food," as we can imagine, can give us an even greater sense of fullness of life, joy, and energy and help to transform ourselves into what we should be in Reality. *"The night is nearly over; the day is almost here. So let us put aside the deeds of darkness and put on the armor of light"* (Rom 13:12).

When the light comes, darkness disappears. It does not need fighting between them. Darkness cannot exist in fullness of light. When we are in a dark room, we do not see everything what is in it. But when the light is on, we can see more. The picture we see in the lighted space is much more detailed. The Light of God is an invincible weapon against darkness. What is darkness? It is a state of low intensity of the inner spiritual light. This does not allow us to get the correct information about the picture of the world within and around us. Darkness is an internal energy state that makes us "through seeing do not see, through hearing do not hear and do not understand." Lack of Light energy inside misleads us, making us blind, deaf, and misperceiving the world. Spiritual Light, when we attract it, invoke it, brings life force with it. Where the Spiritual Light shines, life becomes complete. Humanity, living in darkness for a long time, sees only a tiny part of the picture of the world. It's not good to live without adequate lighting. Thinking that what we see is a realistic and complete picture, humanity commits wrong deeds, deeds of darkness. In order to "ignite the Light," a person needs to consciously introduce this idea or image of the Light of God into the soil of his soul and, through an effort of will, hold it there and make sure that it is not eaten and destroyed by our other desires and thoughts. At first glance it seems completely absurd that mental imagery and conscious control have any value for us. But in fact, they are one of the main components of the spiritual world. After all, the invisible real world consists of mental images of God. In fact, our consciousness should be filled only with what God has put into us. But humanity took its own path, separated from God, and as a result, man created in his consciousness his own ideas about the nature of the world and about himself. So, in our consciousness, where only God's images and ideas should have existed, false ideas and images created by ourselves appeared. Feelings of guilt, suffering, pain, envy, hatred, etc., filled the human mind. But our body is a sacred soil for the seeds of our desires, thoughts, words and feelings, clothed in images. *"Put on the Light of God"* means to sow this image in the soul and surround yourself with this image. This is not some fantasy or deception about something that does not exist. It reminds us of what has always been ours. It's just that what we kept in some distant closet for a very long time, didn't open it for centuries and forgot what we had in it. We've always had it. We could use this knowledge, but even when we remind ourselves of it, we immediately forget it because of the many material concerns in our lives. They, like weeds, crowd out and kill all the other "seeds" that are useful to us. Because of this, we need to remind ourselves that this Spiritual Light has always been, and will be ours forever and ever. No one can do it for us, only ourselves. The farther the object is from the light source, the lower its illumination and the higher its density. Closer means more energy and less density of the object. At some closed distance to the light source each form is so saturated with the power of light that it cannot exist in any other state than in the form of a mental image or word. According to scientific knowledge, the form of any object depends on some circumstances of its existence. Example: since the temperature on the surface of the Sun is about 6000 degrees Celsius, all elements and any rocks, due to such a high temperature, can only exist in a gaseous state. So, the "image" is also one of the forms of light energy and is not an absurdity but a true reality. I think the Creator has prepared for His Sons a place on the border of the Kingdom of God and the beginning of the Kingdom of Darkness. The Sons of God, receiving an abundance of Divine Spiritual Light, were filled to the brim with the Life Energy of the Kingdom of God and the reflected light from the sphere of the beginning of darkness. They ate the best food in the entire Universe. I think the Kingdom of God can be compared to some extent to the most incredible diamond. If diamond is a source of light, then the Kingdom of God radiates and is the most significant source of "God's Light", Life and Love. For God, for His Light, nothing is impossible or insurmountable. The sons of God, being overflowed with vital energy, had to give part of it to the world of darkness, enlightening this world and sharing true knowledge with it. They returned part of this energy to the Kingdom of God. Illuminating the darkness with God's light of Love and Life, the Sons of God through "Divine God's Alchemy" transformed darkness, chaos, complete ignorance and misunderstanding into an incredible world of bliss, joy and happiness and thereby increased and expanded "the size" of the Body of God. The Alchemy of Divine Light provides energy for spiritual growth, and can also, under certain conditions, transform not only the spiritual, but also the material body into an immortal, crystalline one, cleanse it and free it from everything alien to it, turning a person into who he should be. But once the Sons of God left the kingdom of Light and entered the kingdom of darkness, where a person knows much less about his spiritual nature. In a world of low energies humanity would simply dissolve. But God, in His mercy, saved people by creating bodies for them – the "leather clothes". Without "leather clothes" in the vast world of low-frequency energy a person would simply dissolve and disappear. But our Creator gave us a chance to survive. By using willpower, a person can stay alive and even transform into the "true person" that he is. Life in the "cocoon" of the body allows a person to cultivate spiritual fruit inside the body and develop spiritually. This is a chance for us to raise our internal energy to a level sufficient for someone to jump over, and someone else to find a way out of "darkness" into the Kingdom of Light, to our true home.

Documentary and very informative film "What the bleep do we know?" says that a person cannot see, understand and realize anything what was not written and does not exist in his spiritual-visual center, located in the central part of the brain next to the pituitary gland. The scientists in this film have named this center the Observer. Yogis call it the third eye. The American Indians, according to scientists in this film, could not see the English ships plying back and forth in the coastal zone of the ocean when they first appeared before their eyes. They had never seen ships before. Such a form was never registered in their minds and, therefore, did not exist for them. But over time, they began to distinguish the fuzzy outlines of these ships. After a while, they saw them as clearly as the British. Why? If a person regularly sees, hears, or thinks about something, then all these signals are recorded by the Observer in the spiritual center of his brain. When the recorded information becomes strong enough, it becomes "real," visible, and audible for a person in the material world.

Another example: when we read a book for the first time, we rarely get the full information contained in it. If we read the same book a second time, we usually learn much more from it. It even seems like we are reading this for the first time. The American writer Carnegie often said in his books that if someone wants to get complete information from a book, he must read it at least a hundred (or so) times. Constant repetition of the same signals is deposited in our internal memory. Signals superimposed on each other are amplified. We don't know how this happens. But when the signal level in our internal system reaches a certain value, it becomes completely recorded in the Observer and "alive" for us. The Divine Light was recorded in our inner memory from the beginning of creation, but has lost its power. We have forgotten about spiritual bread, caring only about material bread (with a butter). If we retain the image of the Divine

Light within ourselves, its signals, superimposed on each other, can gain strength within the Observer. This is one of the ways given to us for salvation, so that we can transform ourselves from a mortal into an immortal state and have a chance to one day become Sons of the Living God again.

The chemical reaction called diffusion is well known in the scientific world. When two or more chemical substances come into direct contact, they penetrate each other with their chemical elements and create a new chemical body from their two (or more). The newly formed body (their child) will have the characteristics of the bodies of two (or more) parents. As we said earlier, there are no significant differences between the visible and invisible worlds, except for their energy state and state of density of forms. The same reaction, called diffusion, occurs when something invisible to us, such as an image, thought, idea, word or feeling, comes into contact with a similar form from the invisible world or with the gross matter of the body. An image or idea penetrates a material form upon their direct contact and transforms it into a more perfect one (or worse, depending on the idea). The material form takes on the characteristics of both parents. Knowing this, everyone has a chance to take a big step forward. Light and its energy fill everything with life. If its power is sufficient, the gross matter of the body can absorb individual photons and they continue to live inside the body as its integral part illuminating, enlightening, and strengthening the entire internal system of the body. All famous saints are depicted with radiance around their head and body. Their "bodies" were so saturated with photons of God's Light that Light became part of their "bodies". The remains of the Saints after their "physical" death keep this Light, capable of healing the sick. The intense stress we live under weakens our vitality. This makes our bodies so dense that they resist the flow of Divine Light.

Today everyone knows that every living cell in the body has a membrane. If this membrane is clean, it can detect the slightest breath or the subtlest ether signal and respond to it. If this shell has hardened like a rock, then it can only respond to the vibrations of the rough "material" world and does not respond to the subtlest ethereal vibrations of the Spirit. The human body is somewhat similar to a membrane apparatus. It must capture and vibrate in unison with the slightest spiritual manifestations of our desires, feelings, thoughts and images, strengthening and transmitting them to the Universe. Our bodies, contaminated with beliefs and desires alien to us, have lost the ability to capture the subtlest vibrations of the inner Spiritual Self and the Universe. Such a dense membrane is capable of perceiving only vibrations of the rough "material" world. If we lived in a world where clouds cover the entire sky and the sun was not visible for a long time, one would think that the sun does not exist. But it's not right! The invisible and forgotten sun is there, behind the clouds. The sun exists! The same thing happens with the Divine Essence. It is inside each of us. But the dark shadows of "ignorance" have covered this and keep us in darkness. Our essence, the essence of God is within us. It is eternal and unchanging. This Essence does not depend on our knowledge or ignorance of it. It lives inside us and everywhere. Without striving to awaken and know our True Self, we thereby doom ourselves to suffering, pain and illness, not only in this life, but also in many of our reincarnations. The spiritual light of the Father is our true food. The Bible says: *"You are the light of the world"* (Matthew 5:14).

Manifestation and Characteristics of the Essence of the Universe

All religious teachings, philosophical theories and myths of different nations include several basic ideas about God and His Essence. God, according to all teachings, exists forever and is perfect, unchanging, indivisible and the only real Essence in the entire Universe. The Bible says: *"God is Spirit"* (John 4:21) and *"God is light"* (1 John 1:5).

In the previous chapter we talked about the similarity between solar and Divine Light. Knowing the characteristics of sunlight, we tried to determine what qualities "Divine Light" may have. "Divine Light," like any other light, is radiant energy and comes from the very centre of the Universe, which we call God. In ancient Greek philosophy, the Essence of God was called Logos. They considered Him to be Reason, Law and Ruler of the world, determining everything that happens in it. Logos, in their opinion, periodically flashes up and goes out. At the moment of flash, the world arises from His Fire and returns to Him when it goes out. We know that sunlight, focused at one point, creates fire, as does Logos. Since man is the image and likeness of God, his mind must have the same quality as the mind of God. So, a person's mind should determine everything that happens in his life. God is also "Spirit". But how to define the concept of "Spirit?" To do this, let's look at man, who is the image and likeness of God. Spirit and Light are two concepts that cannot be separated from each other, like the concepts of fire and its heat. Unfortunately, man, the image and likeness of God, time ago has ceased to manifest himself as such. He filled himself with desires and feelings that are not in the Divine nature. This is why the thoughts it emits from its centre are different from those emitted by the Divine Light. If God is only perfect Love, "Yes" and "Amen", then in the spiritual nature of man there are many other negative thoughts radiations (or impurities). The resulting strength of these two radiations determines a person's mood or, in other words, his mental and emotional state.

Since any radiation is light energy, it has a wave nature, characterized by wavelength and radiation strength. Desires, feelings and corresponding to them thoughts express the emotional and mental state of a person at every given moment of his life. So, to get an idea of the Spirit of God, let's look at a person's mood, which can be "good", "bad" or anything in between. If the mood is "bad," it is usually associated with negative emotional and mental experiences and is often easily noticeable. Such negative experiences form an inner heaviness in the human soul. According to the intensity of the radiation of such a mood, people can conclude: "It is better not to talk to him now," or "It is better to stay away from him," or "A person needs a couple of kind words." A "good" mood evokes only positive feelings, such as love, happiness, joy, contentment, etc. For someone who has fallen in love for the first time, such feelings are manifested in their entirety with such a tremendous force that, finding no more place inside, they fly out of him like bullets and penetrate deeply into everything and everyone around. The eyes of a lover shine, the face cannot help but smile, and the body glows with love, warmth, happiness and joy. Everyone around can't help but smile back. His mood permeates everything around him, filling with joy and happiness. It's nice to be around someone who is in such love. A person overflowed with such a feeling of love is, as it were, like God. God is the pure Spirit of unchanging Love for everything and everyone. There is nothing in God's Spirit but perfect love and joy. I would say that a person who truly fell in love for the first time is a kind of image and likeness of God. He radiates the Light of Love to everything and everyone. After all, our Creator breathed into the nostrils of man (and, therefore, into us) His Spirit of pure Love. In the human Spirit there was nothing except the Spirit of God, no admixture of other desires, feelings and thoughts. Man, his body, was created only as an instrument for realizing through him the plans and ideas of the Creator. Man, through his ignorance, created in himself another mind, another leader and ruler of his life, who lied to him all the time. This leader did not know how to properly use and manage the human system. After some time, the strengthened "second mind" took complete control over the person. After all, the human body is "living" soil. The negative feelings and thoughts, contained within, grow in our body like a grain grows from the soil of the earth. The internal structure of a person is capable of giving life and nourishment to any feelings, ideas and desires. They, like seeds, grow inside our body without our understanding that we ourselves have sowed them inside ourselves. In the beginning, man was strong enough to protect himself from the temptations of the outer dark world. The darkness could not even get close to the man of that time. Nothing and no one could change the internal structure of a person except... himself. He was the most powerful being on earth. Only he and nobody else could destroy his (and our) internal system. He, due to his ignorance, took advantage of this power and, having sowed in himself desires alien to him, became much weaker. God's desires and those of a liar, always operate in different directions. Their resulting force takes a person away from the Kingdom of God, where humanity has to live all the time in dissatisfaction, pain, suffering and misfortune. However, since no one but man can destroy his inner system, no one but him can restore it. Humanity has thereby weakened itself so much that it currently has no strength to resist any temptations from the outside world. And all this happened only because a person, deceived in his vision of the world and himself, unknowingly took for himself not his own name, but "borrowed", a name with characteristics completely alien to him. This "borrowed" name has become a true reality for him and now he constantly lives under this name, endowing himself more and more with new characteristics of this name, thereby, weakening his vitality. The desires, feelings and ideas of God are so strong and perfect that despite the fact that they have a vibrational nature, they manifest themselves not as vibrations, but as a constant field. The feelings and thoughts of a person who identifies himself with the name body have a low-frequency vibrational nature. The vibration frequency of God's field is so high that there is no gap between the waves. Nothing but Love, Yes and Amen, can penetrate and interact with His higher power. Negative feelings and thoughts spiritually (or energetically) lead humanity away from the Kingdom of God into a land of lower energy. Now we live in a world with a different energy level, far from the Kingdom of God. We moved, I would say, "abroad", to another energy country. Jesus Christ told us the parable of the prodigal son. I think the story of the prodigal son is the story of all humanity, which, as a whole, was and is the "prodigal son of God." Here's the story:

"There was a man who had two sons; The younger one said to his father: "Father, give me my share of the estate." So, he divided his property between them. Not long after that, the younger son got together all he had set off for a distant country and there squandered his wealth in wild living. After he had spent everything, there was a severe famine in that whole country, and he began to be in need. So, he went and hired himself out to a citizen of that country, who sent him to his fields to feed pigs. He longed to fill his stomach with the pods that the pigs were eating, but no one gave him anything. When he came to his senses, he said, "How many of my father's hired men have food to spare, and here I am starving to death! I will set out and go back to my father and say to him: Father, I have sinned against heaven and against you. I am no longer worthy to be called your son; make me like your hired men." So he got up and went to his father. But while he was still a long way off, his father saw him and was filled with

compassion for him; he run to his son, threw his arms around him, and kissed him. The son said to him: "Father! I have sinned against heaven and against you. I am no longer worthy to be called your son." But the father said to his servants: "Quick! Bring the best robe and put it on him. Put a ring on his finger, and sandals on his feet. Bring the fattened calf and kill it. Let's have a feast and celebrate. For this my son of mine was dead and is alive again; he was lost and is found. So, they began to celebrate. Meanwhile, the older son was in the field. When he came near the house, he heard music and dancing. So, he called one of the servants and asked him what was going on. "Your brother has come," he replied, "and your father killed the fattened calf because he has him back safe and sound." The older brother became angry and refused to go in. So, his father went out and pleaded with him. But he answered his father, "Look! All these years I've been slaving for you and never disobeyed your orders. Yet you never gave me even a young goat so I could celebrate with my friends. But and when this son of yours who has squandered your property with prostitutes comes home, you killed the fattened calf for him!" "My son," the father said, "you are always with me, and everything I have is yours. But we had to celebrate and be glad because this brother of yours was dead and is alive again; he was lost and is found". (Luke 15: 11-32).

The world we live in is not just a place on land like America, China or other parts of our planet. The world also consists of layers (or countries) that differ from each other in energy levels. A light bulb is a light source similar to any other sources of light energy. The power of light at its center is so great that darkness simply cannot exist there. The farther from the center, the light intensity decreases, scattering over wider spatial spheres. It's the same with Divine light. The energy at its source exceeds in illumination all other places more distant from the center. At some distance from the center is the Kingdom of God (third sphere). The state of consciousness, feelings and thoughts there is "Love", happiness, "Yes!" and "Amen". This energy level is so high that nothing lower in energy can penetrate or even come close to it. Selfishness and all non-divine desires push a person out of the Kingdom of God into countries of a lower energy level. Changing desires and thoughts back to higher ones can return a person to the land of higher energies. Feelings, ideas and thoughts are energies that manifest as wave vibrations. Each energetic sphere of God's Light has a specific range of wavelengths in which certain feelings, ideas and thoughts have energetic food and can exist. When the Prodigal Son wished to see the world outside the Kingdom of his Father, he imagined that somewhere out there, in foreign lands, there was another more interesting life and that magical adventures awaited him there. He allowed this unrealistic, deceptive idea to seep into his mind and take over his imagination. He had a desire to get to know this country. Nothing would have happened to him if he had immediately gotten rid of this desire. But for some time he kept this desire in his mind and thus nourished this idea with his higher internal energy, giving it food for growth. Then, when this desire became strong enough, he decided to fulfill it. All the time he thought only about his desire to see another world outside the kingdom of his Father. Thus, roughly speaking, he limited the world of his interests from the highest to the smallest, and in time began to see, hear and understand that what was part of his limited interest. When he left his father's house, all the spiritual treasures and "riches" that belonged to him by birth were in him and with him. He went to an unknown country, having inherited from his Father all the Highest Divine energy. At first, as you might guess, he enjoyed his adventure, moving further and further away from his home. He had the fullness of God's spiritual power. This made him feeling happy. Using this power, he could have whatever he wanted for a limited time. But there was no proper (energetic) food for his soul in this country. Slowly, step by step, he squandered all the wealth of his Spiritual Powers. The desires he desired were objects of the outside world, different from those he had in his own country. Holding them in his thoughts, he fed them with his inner spiritual energy. This made him weaker and weaker. So his ever-decreasing internal energy carried him farther and farther from his native country, from brighter places to darker ones. Once he found himself in a country with such low energy that he lost all the wealth received from his father, and he was starving. God, by His mercy, saved humanity from death, as we said earlier, by isolating its inner Divine Essence from the lower energy world where humanity had slipped, by placing it in a bodily form. Our highest internal spiritual energy would dissolve and disappear in a world alien to us without the insulating protection of the body. Therefore, even if we have used up all our spiritual power, a small part, the germ, DNA, always remains inside, giving us a chance to restore our true nature. So, after some time wandering abroad, the prodigal son found himself penniless and was forced to hire himself as a servant to some evil man, living with pigs and eating their food. He had to work a lot in this country. By origin he was the son of a king, but in a foreign country he worked as a slave for cruel people. His interest in the outside world led him to a country where pigs were his best friends. During this difficult time, he thought only about how good it was for him to live in His Father's house. The ideas of God, filled with higher energy, nourish everything and everyone with an abundance of life, correct knowledge of the whole world, and give willpower to control all the functions of oneself. Any thought and desire other than God's ideas automatically places a person in a country with a lower energy level. They allow other low-frequency waves to penetrate them and introduce many "viruses". "Viruses" change the strength, shape and direction of perceived signals and the operation of the entire system, just as it happens in a computer. False information automatically transfers a person from the Kingdom of God to a foreign energy country.

No one drives a person out of his true home, but a person leaves the Kingdom of God, without even knowing it, of his own free will.

The Mind

I think that once upon a time, before man violated the commandments of God, there was only one World (God's) Mind. When God created man from a clay, a man-clay was just an inanimate statue without any desires, feelings or thoughts. When God breathed His breath with all its contents into the nostrils of this statue, the clay-man became alive, gaining feelings, desires and thoughts. There was nothing in an alive man except the Spirit of God, His desires, ideas, images and thoughts. So, man has become not only the image and likeness of God, but also the place where God lives. When man violated the commandments of God, he saw himself as a separate from his true Divine Essence and God form. Believing what he saw, and having an internal structure capable of giving life to any of his desires and thoughts, he voluntarily created another mind within himself that deceived and manipulated him. This deceptive mind began to guide his actions and his further development. The Divine Spirit and the deceptive mind in man are always working in different directions. The resultant of these two forces is always weaker. It weakens a person spiritually and physically. All sacred scriptures, sages and religious teachings describe the nature of God as the World Universal Mind with its manifestation as Light containing Life, Love, all Good, Yes and Amen. They also consider Him to be the Lawgiver and Ruler of the world, determining everything that happens in it. The world, in their opinion, arises from this Mental Light Fire and disappears with Its extinction. According to their concepts, God manifests Himself as Mental Fire. If it is so, what creates this fire? Temperature? But the God's Mind is present everywhere and in everything, including our bodies. In this case, our bodies would be burn at temperatures above 41 degrees Celsius. Thus, Divine fire is not from high temperatures. This Light, as I think, is the light of thoughts or mental images of the Creator. Just as sunlight concentrated at one point sets fire to a wooden board, so Mental Fire is the concentration of all thoughts, ideas and images of God at one point, where it manifests as the Fire of mental power but of a different nature when sunlight. The light of thought, concentrated at one point, diverging from it into space, "draws" the World, directs, creates and determines everything that happens in it. It is the most powerful force on our planet and the entire Universe. According to its characteristics and manifestations thought is a vector quantity. Thought does not come to us by itself. It's directly connected with our desires and determines according to their strength our actions for its fulfillment. As soon as there is a desire, the thought immediately comes to mind to fulfill this desire. I would say, no one single desire can exist for a long without thought energy. The desire disappears if the thought does not connect to it. Thought in the form of light is a mental energy that carries and gives life force or life to everything. Determined by our desires, thoughts rule and determine our actions. A man, depending on his desires, can be God like or evil like. It all depends on the type of our desires and thoughts. It doesn't matter what desire we choose: "good" or "bad," "kind" or "evil." In this case, associated with a thought in the human mind, a desire transmits its vibrations to thought. Thought picks it up and, strengthening them, carries them directly into the Universe. The Divine Essence lives within man, whether we realize it or not. This is our basis and real inner content. It gives life to everything that we sow in our desires and thoughts. God Himself fulfilled all His desires. He gave man the same freedom to choose desires. Thus, everything that we feel and think, good or bad, can become our distorted or true reality. Information that misleads us, such as words, advertisements, images, desires or anything else that enters our consciousness, penetrates and accumulates in our consciousness on a daily basis. These signals, superimposed on each other, over time become so strong that can become as real to us as it was real to our ancestors that the shape of the Earth is a flat plate. All right and good has been introduced to our system by our Creator, and all of this is of a great benefit to us. Repeating every day a few kind words, given to us by the Creator, can give a significant positive result. The right mantra or prayer is not only good for daily repetition, but also necessary. Several desires simultaneously generate the same number of thoughts for their fulfillment. Since every thought is a force and it has its own direction, the resultant of all these forces most often destroys our mind and our entire being as a whole. One desire and one thought, like a lens, can transmit our desire multiplied by the mind to the Forces of the Universe for its fulfillment. If everything is done correctly, then what we ask for should be given to us in visible form, say the sages. The thought is the source of energy for absolutely everything. The seed of desire, sown in the soil of the human soul, develops in a way unknown to us. The desire that we keep in our hearts and minds, gradually gaining strength, turns from an invisible form into a material one, visible to us. Everything visible comes from the hidden source of all the invisible forces of life and wisdom. To be fulfilled, a desire must have specific power, say the sages. If there is a strong desire, a thought immediately arises and acts to deliver it to the Universe for fulfillment. The relationship between thought and desire is in some similarity to the organization of government power. Desire plays the role of legislator. Thought is the executive body responsible for the execution of the Law. Let's say the desire a man has is completely vital. In this case, thought, which has enormous reserves and strength for its implementation, gives to it the right direction and provides all the forces at its disposal to convey this desire to the Higher Powers of the Universe (or God). Without these (God's) powers we cannot create anything real. If the desire, say, is not very strong, for example, we would not mind drinking some water, then, thinking about something else, we forget about this desire until we find water to drink. The mind does not work with weak desires. Sometimes the desire to drink becomes so strong that we forget about everything and think only about water. In this case, the connection between thought and desire can become so strong that it can simply pulsate through our body, banishing all other thoughts and desires from the mind. In this case, we give up all other desires and search for water until we satisfy this desire. If we want water, but are well aware that we cannot find it for a long time, then separating thought from desire can help us remain without water for a long time. Even if we see water somewhere, thinking about something else, we may forget about our desire to drink. This is because at this moment our mind is occupied with other ideas. Desire disappears almost instantly if thought does not connect with it. Thought is the mental energy that feeds desires, images, feelings, etc. Without sufficient mental nutrition, none of the desires can last long. Desires, like thoughts, have a vibrational nature, but do not have sufficient strength and cannot be directed in the right direction of the Universe. Only thought has such qualities and power. Without thought they dissolve and disappear. Nowadays, humanity is well-versed in nourishing the body, knowing the ingredients, counting calories and choosing more fresh organic fruits and vegetables. This is, of course, necessary. We know that our bodies are made of what we eat, right? If we drink carrot or beet juice for some time, our skin, urine, and even saliva will take on the color of carrots or beets. But we are not so concerned about the spiritual food we choose, which is much more important. Our spirit, like our body, is what we feed it with. We often feed our spirit by doing things we enjoy in the material world, such as watching crime or horror films. Some of our children have been playing computer games with images of murder, fighting and evil almost since the day they were born. We choose all this because our desires are always connected with the outside world. The weakened spiritual power of a person does not have enough strength to break the shell of forms and come into contact with their spiritual content. This encourages us in every possible way to eat food for "pigs" and "slaves." We are constantly spiritually not in our "kingdom", which is located inside us, but in the external world, where darkness reigns, where there is no proper energy food for the Sons of the Living God. We are doing what the prodigal son did when he left his country. If we try to spend three days only in joy, it will overwhelm us to such an extent that it will be impossible to contain it within. Joy will beat and shoot out of us. If we are in a state of a melancholy and sadness for a long time and do not try to switch or forget the "reason" for this mood by doing some work or reminding ourselves of some pleasant moments, then we can reach a state leading to suicide. As I already said, thought is a vector quantity characterized by its module, direction and point of application. A thought can either harm or benefit a human being. If our desires and thoughts jump back and forth like mad horses, then the resulting force will be close to zero or will have a negative effect. I think this is the only reason why Jesus Christ said:

"Whoever is not with Me is against me, and whoever does not gather with me, he is scattered." (Matthew 12:30)

If we do not collect life force every moment, we lose it in this alien for ourselves world. A person with many desires is spinning in the whirlpool of these desires and thoughts, wasting his life force. The one who seeks the Truth follows the path indicated to us by Jesus Christ, goes to the Father, to the Light, to Life by that narrow path, where only one desire and one thought prevails over all the others - to be one with the Father. The program for the fulfillment of any desire is in our internal system and in the system of the entire Universe. So, as we said earlier, our desire can be our best friend or our worst enemy. It all depends on the type of desires that we put into our internal system. If we are sad, our entire internal intellectual system reinforces this sadness, considering it to be our heart's desire. In this case, our body begins to produce chemical elements that will work to strengthen this condition. When we are happy, our internal organs work to make us even happier. When we want or need something, our internal system works to enhance that feeling or desire. This is one of our principles of "Divinity." If a person is well aware that the body becomes what we feed it with, then it would be great to realize that the spirit also becomes what we feed and fill it with. Our actions are a continuation and extension of our inner desires and thoughts and, therefore, ourselves into the world, making us "bigger" or "smaller", depending on our choices. We increase or decrease ourselves in the material or spiritual world. Our affairs are like plants. They grow out of us, uniting us with the deceptive or Real world into a single organism. The world we live in forces us to have many desires at the same time. We need to pay bills, buy a dress for our daughter's wedding, win the lottery, prepare for a meaningful conversation at work, etc. This creates a whirlwind of thoughts in our mind. For many, it is almost impossible to hold one thought in your head for even two minutes. Why? I think this is because we, as spiritual beings, love and desire what we are not. Since we, humanity, find ourselves in a world that is alien to us, our thoughts are always focused and connected with this that is not in our world. Being spiritual, we love and want to have many objects from the material world alien to us, regardless of their spiritual content. Our physical eyes love and want to have them in physical forms. But we are Spiritual beings and can unite into a single organism only with spiritual substances through Spirit with Spirit. On the other hand, we often try, through love, to unite into an integral system with external forms of the world that are alien to us, without taking into account their internal spiritual content. This is impossible. We can't just make one whole bucket out of two or more without melting them and changing shape. But the spirit of God, the only one living in all forms, only He can unite everything into one whole through life and love. After all, all spirits, "good" or "bad," came from one source - the life force of God. "Good" Spirit feeds on the Divine Essence and gives it energy for the growth of goodness and prosperity. The people who created all the "bad" spirits give them food from their own Divine Spirit that lives within them. Thus, the nurture the "bad" spirits is in some way partly Divine. Thus, we weaken ourselves by feeding "evil" with our Divine Essence. Whether we realize it or not, we were, are and always will be spiritual beings. Our name is "Son of God," and not at all the one that we, out of our ignorance, took or "borrowed" for ourselves. The Divine Spirit lives in the material vessel of our body and is our true nature and the true "I Am". Our bodies cannot be one with bodies of any other form. But our spirit can communicate with the spirits of different objects and become one through contact and love. Thoughts are the determining factor in human life. We may say that our mind is our ruler or king who determines everything in our lives. A good ruler or king of the country, if he wants to govern the country properly, must be in his country with his subjects. If he is somewhere far abroad, robbers from all over the world can quickly come and steal all the treasures of his state. Our mind, "our king ", spends most of the time in an external, alien to us "foreign" world, and not at home, inside the body, in our own country. When the ruler is not in the country, the population does not know him and forgets about his existence. They have no one to turn for help, and criminals freely rob the country and its people. There is only one way to clear the mind of many thoughts. It is to return to its realm which is in our bodies. *"Don't you know that you are the temple of God and the Spirit of God lives in you?* (1 Cor: 3-16). Our body is the temple of God who lives in it. Spirit of God presents everywhere. But the closest place of His presence for us is within us, in His temple, in our bodies. *"He, God, is nearer than breath"* says the Bible. We don't have to go far to find God. Directing thoughts into the body, uniting with our true spiritual "I am," we should pray to God and with God in His temple, inside our body. We cannot be heard without combining our desire and thought with our spiritual selves. God does not know us as a body. He knows us as part of His spirit and hears only it. Jesus Christ said that we have to pray to Him with all our being, mind, heart, soul, and all strength "in His Temple." That means to do it in our body. Only there, concentrating thoughts together with Him at one point, we with Him can send them to the Universe for fulfillment. Long ago, there were special requirements for the construction of temples. It was a very high dome. When people prayed in the temple, the vibrations of their prayers were concentrated and collected, like the sun's rays collected by a lens, into a metal dome. Collected, they had to go out in the form of vibrations into the Universe, to God for their fulfillment. The purpose of the church was to convey the requested information to the Universe. If you look at the human body, you can find similarities in its structure with sacred temples. Our heads are like a high dome. When we pray, all the forces of our inner organism, everything inside must unite and concentrate at one point in a head. Previously, there was only one king in the country. He called on the entire population of the country to come to church on the chosen day and pray together so that their prayers would be strong enough to be heard. If our body is a temple, and our mind is a ruler, then the mind must call on the entire population of the country, to everyone in it, to come and pray together to God within the body. Jesus Christ said: *"Love the Lord your God with all your heart, with all your soul, with all your strength, and with all your mind; Love your neighbor as yourself."* (Luke 10:27). He also told us to be persistent in prayer. Love and joy are the only feelings in the Essence of God and His Kingdom.

Therefore, we need to come to God with love for Him and pray with Him, having only one desire. The concentration of all forces occurs in the "dome" located in the brain. Eastern masters call this place the third eye. It has a direct connection with the Universe. Only the Divine Essence within us, in interaction with the same Divine Essence of the entire Universe, can fulfill our request. The body is just a tool for establishing this contact. Only when the Divine Being who lives in us and who is real "I am" asks God, we together with him and only through him will be able to receive what we ask for. If "with our body," without the participation of the Divine essence within us, we say: "Let there be more red blood cells in my blood," this will not happen. Both internal and external systems do not obey the body's commands. They do not know and do not recognize the body as their master. But the entire system will unerringly execute the same command if it comes from that Spiritual Being who makes all decisions within us. Only he has such a higher power, to which everything inside our body unquestioningly obeys. This intelligent being in each of us, as well as in the entire Universe, is our true "I Am." We should train ourselves to do everything with that intelligent Being and gradually become one with Him and be Him. The body system executes His commands accurately and without delay. Our decision-making True Self has unerring control over all of our internal systems, which are His and our own. He knows very well what is best to do in any situation. If there is a viral infection, he immediately regulates how many white and red blood cells should be in the blood, how many and what types of hormones should be produced, what temperature and blood pressure should be, etc. And all our internal systems immediately follow these commands, never ignore them, and does everything without errors. His orders are always the best for our whole being at any moment. The material body, being in a state of strong tension due to the load on it of tasks that are beyond its strength, shrinks, acquires hardness and gives us incorrect commands, which we immediately carry out. Our organism is a priceless living Universe, consisting of countless living cells, various microorganisms, tissues that make up the organs of the body, and thanks to their harmonious interaction, we exist. We do not always "consciously or mentally" understand that our liver or any other part or cell within the body is part of me and is "I am". And we often act against our own organs by eating the wrong food and not changing the bad habits of life. It means I, myself, act against myself. My liver, my cell, or any part of me is Me, and I am my liver, my cell, and I am any part of me. My state depends on how each cell and organ within me work and interact with the overs. Their interaction is completely dependent on my interaction with each of them. To get to know someone better, you need to communicate and spend more time with them. After all, all relationships develop only through contact and communication. The primary task of a person, as I think, is to establish contact with his inner system and become her friend. We, all of humanity and the whole world are a single organism. We are not separate from each other and are part of the Body and Essence of God. Therefore, we have every right to say: "I am part of the body of God and therefore I am He. God is in all parts of me; therefore, God is I am, and I am is He." We must treat every organ, cell and tissue of our inner being and every creature in this Universe as well as we treat God. If we do not want to harm ourselves, we should not harm any organ or cell of our body and the Universal system. All parts of the Universe were created in a certain image and likeness of God. Unfortunately, we often treat our internal system as ruthlessly as a planter treats his slaves. Most of the time we are not inside the body in which the "I am" lives. Our thoughts are always in the outside world. But not bad to remember we are there where our thoughts are. The visible world, in which we find ourselves, thanks to our thoughts, offers us many seductive and attractive things. Thoughts, under the influence of many desires and impressions, are spinning wildly in our heads, not allowing the power of thought to manifest itself with sufficient force. Wandering in a material world alien to us, where we are slaves, we must not forget about our true origin. By birth and blood, we are all Sons of our Heavenly Father. We left our father's house of our own free will, but we can always return. It was not difficult to leave home with all our spiritual and physical treasures. But after we've squandered them, the journey home won't be easy. Mental and physical adversity, weakness and suffering await us. In order to somehow make the path home easier, spiritual sages recommend that we do not dive deeply into this world, remembering that we are in it temporarily, only passing through it to our eternal home. Have you ever noticed that when we pray, we do it instinctively with our eyes closed. With our eyes closed, the world of temptations disappears and temporarily does not exist for us. Of course, we can't completely ignore everything we're going through. But it's not bad to remember: we're just passing through this world. Everything in it is transitory, appears and after a while disappears, passes by us and flies away. It's like clouds that appear and disappear in the sky after a while. The realization that our nature is eternal, and life in this body is only a part of our eternal life without beginning and end, can help us pass through everything that comes our way, good or bad, calmly, look at this world spiritually from the inside, focusing attention and thoughts only on the eternal, on the Light and Love of our Father, seeing in everything only the Divine Essence which gives life and love to everything, contains absolute knowledge and correct understanding of oneself and Reality. Divine Light is stored in our bodies, as well as throughout the Universe. Since a person has borrowed the name "body", which does not correspond to his nature, and lives according to the laws of this body, the compacted body, due to excessive load on it, cannot catch the subtlest internal high-frequency vibrations from our true Self. This creates increasing dissonance in the work of the entire internal system of the body. So, we have seeded and created within ourselves another entity that deceives us, the mind of the liar, and we have allowed two different minds to live within us. We know well one of them who deceives us by saying that we are just material bodies. We hardly know the other, true invisible Divine Essence. Two essences - two masters or two "kings" inside us. In practice, most often we choose the one we know and love the most, the body. We "worship" him by following all his commands. On the other hand, the Universe knows and communicates only with that invisible spiritual being in us who makes all sinless decisions within our body. The Universe does not respond to the commands of our material body. Because of our misconceptions, it is very condensed and distorts all the information that we receive about the world and about ourselves. If the body is cleared of delusions, then light will pass through it more intensely and the photons captured and held inside will work. Then our eyes, ears and minds will become more open to better understand things. The more intense the light in the body, the more strongly the light energy of the Universe is attracted and thereby enlightens and strengthens a person, making the "geometry" of his body one with the entire Essence of the Universe.

Great yogis say that in the beginning of spiritual development it is essential to become "whole", so, that the material body vibrations to be in unison with the spiritual "I am." When it's done, the second next step is to separate the thoughts from the emotions and feelings. On the path of life we can encounter the most unexpected situations, sometimes pleasant, more often sad or tragic, causing us negative emotions. The body system takes on all the vibrations of our inner self, including emotions, most often negative (with a low frequency). The best thing we can do to overcome and smooth out all of life's difficulties is not to dive deep into them. To do this, you need to separate thoughts from them, without giving energetic food to such feelings as sadness, despair, disbelief, hopelessness, etc. They do not exist in the true Divine Reality. To do this, we need to reorient our thoughts, separate them from emotions and redirect them in the right direction, from the outside world to the inside. If we can hold positive thoughts within ourselves long enough without "negativity," difficult situations should gradually smooth out and dissipate like smoke. To solve all our problems in the physical world, we must calmly and soberly do everything possible to make them disappear. Spiritual teachers advise us to try to mentally see the situation as having already been successfully resolved, perfect and bright, as if it had already passed. After all, everything in this life is fleeting and transitory. If we remember that we do not just have this small period of life that we are experiencing now, but that we have been given eternal life, without beginning or end, then this can help us calmly pass through everything that comes our way. Our difficult situations are like clouds. They block the Spiritual Light for us, just as clouds block the sunlight, and we find ourselves in the darkness of our consciousness. But it's good to remember that if today a cloud covers the sun and everything around is dark and gloomy, then as soon as the winds blow, whether this cloud wants it or not, the wind picks them up and carries away. The same applies to our difficulties. The brighter our spirit, the brighter our life and the less difficulties. But even when the clouds cover the sky and it gets dark, we continue to go about our daily activities by simply turning on the lights. In brighter light, everything is visible much better and more fully. We can do the same thing by mentally turning on the spiritual light, creating a mental image of pure bright white light inside and around us, or by "putting" the right words about Light into our souls, endowing them with all the properties of Light. Spiritual light is mental in nature and therefore has unlimited power. A mental image can penetrate anywhere, including the situation in which we find ourselves. This light does not need to fight with anyone or anything. It's simple: where there is light, there is no darkness. We can see, by mentally illuminating a situation, how it has improved or even disappeared. When we pray, as we said earlier, we close our eyes. In this way we isolate ourselves from the outside world. After all, the purpose of prayer is to receive spiritual fruit or an answer to your request. When we stop looking at this world with physical eyes, thoughts about it leave us. We are immersed in the inner world of subtler matter, where we can deeply feel the words of prayer so that it will bear "fruit." As I said, the spiritual world is not so different from the "physical" world. In order to have "physical" fruits in the physical world, we must also give up many things to which we are accustomed. A pregnant woman gives up noisy companies, wine and cigarettes, and spends more time in the fresh air and sun. She does all this to give birth to a healthy child. The caterpillar is one of the best examples of dedication to obtain "fruit". She grew up in a big and beautiful world on a green tree. There she had a lot of food, air and friends. But when the time comes to produce offspring, she cuts herself off from this beautiful and big world pulling a silky thread from her stomach and wrapping it around herself. She voluntarily leaves this big beloved world and encloses herself in a dark tiny cocoon in order to fulfill her main purpose on earth. She does this of her own free will. Nobody pushed her to do this. And there, in a cocoon, in complete darkness and isolation, her body begins to transform into a new creation in order to give birth to offspring to continue its kind. If, while in the cocoon, she always thought about the world that she voluntarily left, worrying about how bad it was to lie in darkness and cramped conditions, then all her efforts to fulfill her destiny on earth would have been in vain. But she willingly gives her whole body (and all her desires and thoughts) to transform her body into a butterfly, which, emerging from the cocoon into the wide world, will lay eggs to produce many new caterpillars, which will eventually produce even more butterflies. Interesting, isn't it? It is a life cycle without beginning or end. I think that the process of life without beginning and end is God's plan for the whole world, including man. But, unfortunately, people are different from the rest of the world in many ways. This is because of the two entities within us. All our actions have a two-way effect. Everything that a person creates has two effects: a positive one, which brings some comfort to our lives, and a negative one, which destroys our inner spiritual and physical state. Let's look at the modern idea of using only green energy such as solar panels and wind farms without going into big ideas. These ideas seem to be very good. But solar panels and wind power plants are made from natural and artificial materials. And even their use has a two-way effect: positive and negative. They produce "cleaner" energy. This is a good and big plus. But their service life is limited, and after a while they have to be thrown away or destroyed. Throwing them away means filling our planet with ineradicable garbage. But it is almost impossible to destroy such materials. It takes too much energy to destroy them. These ideas are good for our generation, but will bring many problems to the next. With the passing of our generation, life on the planet continues. Our children and grandchildren will live after us in the same world that we leave them. Life is eternal and has no beginning or end. But we are limited in our vision of the future outcome of what we do. We need everything now, in this life, and we don't think about what will happen after us. But our children and grandchildren will live after us. The examples we have considered are not the worst, but some of the simplest.   When we look at man-made objects such as beautiful buildings, great cars, paintings, listening to music, etc., we cannot help but be amazed at the beauty and wisdom required to create them all. The people are very talented: talented, like God. No one is like us in this world. But the internal sensations created in the soul of each person are very different from what is created by nature and what is created by human hands and minds. Objects created by human hands do not reciprocate us, like those created by nature. The beauty of nature immediately responds to our admiration with the power of mutual love, surpassing our delight. Nature's response to our admiration reaches deep within us, filling us with peace and joy, creating a feeling of "fullness" and bliss as if we had eaten the best food in the world. And it is true. This food is God's Light and Love. This is the best food for everyone. If we admire God's creation, we thereby come into contact with it. Nature knows us well as a part of herself and in return permeates us with what she has, her mutual admiration and Love. We unite with her through mutual Love and become one organism. The Great Essence of love lives in us and in everything that is created by God. It doesn't matter whether we know it or not. When we look at the beauty of nature and admire it, we come into contact with the same Essence of Love and spiritually merge with it. Spiritually, through Love, we are all one body with everything that God has created. We have one Essence, and together we are one living organism. Each part of this organism interacts with another through Love. Jesus Christ said: *"Love your neighbor as yourself."* His words are easy to understand if you know the principle of the integrity of the Universe. The well-being of one living organism depends on the well-being of each of its parts. "I am" is one part of the whole body, and all other organs are one with "I am". Even if we find ourselves in an energetically "alien" country, this does not mean that our nature has changed. Yes, in a "foreign" country we are treated like slaves, but by "blood" we remain Sons of God everywhere and in every situation. The blood of God flows in our veins. A diamond covered with dirt is the same diamond with all its qualities. Clean it and it will shine and be the same as before. Everything created by nature (or the Divine Essence) ideally and harmoniously follows the path of a life cycle that has neither beginning nor end. Everything that a person does is done for his convenience or for the desire to fill his life with something "purely humanly significant" and has a beginning and an end. God, possessing the nature of ideal Love (without impurities, like a diamond), breathed His Spirit of Love into everything He created. Everything turned out perfect and filled with the same God's Spirit of Love. When a person does something, he "breathes" his spirit into it. His nature consists of the Spirit of God and the spirit of separation from the whole world, filled with his selfish ambitions. Two masters with different characters and desires determine his desires. As a result, everything he does has a double effect: positive and negative. While enjoying the surrounding nature, we come into contact with it through the Divine component of our Spirit. In response, having cognized only one feeling of Love, it immediately includes our Divine nature into a single system with itself and sends us what it has: peace, grace and Love. When a person reminds himself of problems in life or at work, his thoughts immediately return him to these problems. At this moment we immediately find ourselves in the world of these problems. The connection with nature is severed and we find ourselves caught up in the issues we think about. We are always where our thoughts are. But even if we stop conscious contact with nature, nature still sends us its Love, but we cease to feel its beneficial influence so strongly. Contact is broken. Conscious communication and contact are essential for spiritual life. Awareness of life's problems and adversities moves us from one energy level of life to another, to where our thoughts are. The mind takes us to where it is, defines and directs our lives.

Thought, space, time, and us

Everything in the world of gross matter exists and lives in space and time, with one exception. For thought or mind there is no space and time. We immediately find ourselves where our mind is. The mind does not need to move or travel through space and time. With the mind we are exactly where the thought is. Thought can take us to the past, where we can experience everything as deeply as in the past. Mentally, we can be transported to the future, to the moon or to any country that we dreamed about or wanted to visit. Mind can be everywhere, in many places at any given time. Mentally, we can get inside the Sun, end up on the Moon, and ride a horse across a rainbow. The mind has no boundaries. For it there is nothing impossible or limited, as for God, for whom there are no limits. Apart from God Himself, no one can control His mind, since there is no one and nothing more perfect and powerful than Him. The same applies to the human mind. Our mind is also the determining factor and master of our life. No one can control a person's thoughts except himself. Using a will, a person can consciously force himself to think and act in the right direction, which our body often resists. We can control our choice of desires and ideas and with their help regulate our feelings, the functioning of the brain, liver, heart, all systems and functions of the body and its cells. But lack of strength often prevents people from managing their lives correctly. Science says we only use 4-5% of our mind's capacity. We typically use willpower to lose weight, improve our financial situation, and get a promotion. We also study foreign languages, read, etc. But, first of all, in order to increase the power of mind and will, we must, I think, educate and teach ourselves to communicate and know our internal system well. Yoga philosophy says that for spiritual development a person needs to know the anatomy of all his organs and their location. Mental contact with each organ and the entire internal system of our inner "I am" can help us prepare the ground for closer friendship, to get to know each other better. After all, all relationships, friendship and love begin with communication. By spending more time together, we get to know each other better. "Know yourself and you will know the whole world" say the sages of the East. After all, every human body is a reduced copy of the entire Universe. We train our muscles by doing many exercises. Just like the physical being, our spiritual being also needs regular and constant training. At first glance, such an activity may seem much more difficult than physical training. But over time this should bear fruit. Exercise benefits the physical body. Doing it we feel better. But do you know that the mind can do the same work for the physical body much faster and more efficiently? For example, if we want to make our biceps more significant, we have to train dumbbells for several months. But the same result can be achieved through spiritual training and without physical activity, say yogis. If a person can mentally give commands to the biceps (or other organs), causing in them the same sensations as during physical activity, then the desired result can be achieved much faster and with greater efficiency. The possibilities of the mind are limitless. With the help of our mind we can improve or even change the condition of our biceps and our entire physical body. The Bible says, *"You all must be born again."* But as far as I understand, we do not need to be spiritually reborn. Our nature and inner being were and remain the same. We were and remain beloved children of the living God. Consciously, mentally, through an effort of will, we are given the opportunity to regenerate our flesh, cleanse it of toxins, fill it with life energy and, as the Bible says, "be born again." The Spirit of God is Light filled with boundless Love. By mentally awakening the feeling of love in the heart and, through an effort of will, holding this feeling inside, we can saturate the body with the energy of Light and even achieve a state in which this Love will take root and constantly live inside the body. Another thing we can do to improve the condition of our body and, therefore better understand ourselves and the world, is to use the knowledge about the qualities of the mind revealed to us by spiritual Masters. This knowledge tells us that the Spirit of God, His Mind, and therefore His light, lives in everything and fills the entire Universe and all its smallest particles. This Great Light lives within us, in our physical and spiritual bodies, organs and cells. It is known that photons from sunlight have enormous power and can transfer their energy to all living beings for growth and development. If the light of the Sun has such power, then it is difficult to imagine what power the Light of God can have. It can be infinitely powerful. By realizing

His power, we can mentally allow Him to freely and easily enter our bodies and move to any place where we mentally direct Him. He does not need to move in space and time. It immediately appears where we need it through conscious contact. It is able to cleanse and restore the lattice structure of the body to maximum strength. Of course, this may seem like a pipe dream. But this dream can come true if you really want it. Even a few minutes of spiritual exercise a day can help us move in this direction. It is advisable not to miss a single day. In everyday life, people can easily forget about spiritual training. Moses once advised his people to wear colored bands on their wrists to remind them of their spiritual nature. Daily spiritual exercises strengthen the entire internal system, and a person may one day achieve such strength that he himself can become a source of Divine Light.

Breathing and Spirituality

The Bible says: *"The Lord God formed man from the dust of the ground and breathed into his nostrils the breath of life, and man became a living being"* (Genesis 2:7). Thus, the breath of God, according to the Bible, turned an inanimate statue of a man into a living being. Before the breath of Life into the clay figurine it could not move, had no feelings or desires, and was only suitable for growing wheat seeds or other plants in its body. But the breath of life breathed into his nostrils made this inanimate statue a living being with all the feelings, desires, ideas, images and dreams that God breathed into him. Through breathing God united the motionless, emotionless statue of man with the subtlest components of the Cosmic Spirit. Only thanks to the breath of life did man (and all of us) become alive. Breathing is a constant connection between our gross material being and the entire body of the Universe or God. This is one of the most important functions of our internal system. Without breathing there is no life for us. There are many opinions and recommendations about the importance of proper breathing. It, like everything else, should be trained. Some, for example, recommend consciously monitoring your breathing. As you breathe in, consciously breathe in the energy of life along with the air; exhaling, also consciously exhale from yourself (radiate) the energy of Love to all creation. This is one of the important exercises for spiritual development. Another important principle of spiritual development is breath holding. When we pray to God or meditate, we usually become mentally aware of the words being spoken, watching them flow through us. In this case, we automatically hold our breath. Just watch yourself. In order to realize and deeply feel what we are praying or meditating about, breathing subconsciously stops temporarily. The energy expenditure for the work of the body at this time decreases, and the energy associated with the spiritual body is released. Holding our breath temporarily helps us forget about the material part of ourselves and give free rein to the spirit within us. God doesn't need to breathe. He provides everything His creatures need, including breathing. It lives everywhere: in the hottest places, such as the Sun, and in the coldest places, such as the depths of the oceans, in vacuum space, etc. Science once again confirms the correctness of the spiritual revelations of the sages about the importance of holding your breath. It turns out that the air we breathe contains a negligible amount of carbon dioxide, only 0.03%. Scientific evidence shows that carbon dioxide is vital and essential for all of us. The body produces it itself by burning glucose in the muscles. Since there is practically no carbon dioxide in the air, we ourselves produce it and receive it during physical activity. Due to a sedentary lifestyle, stress and life difficulties, most people develop deep breathing. When we worry, our heart automatically starts beating faster and our breathing becomes deeper. As the inhalation becomes deeper, the exhalation also becomes stronger and deeper. At the same time, we exhale a lot of carbon dioxide. This leads to insufficient levels of it in the body. Carbon dioxide is a natural vasodilator and catalyst for supplying cells with oxygen. There is enough oxygen in the air. But cells practically do not absorb it without carbon dioxide in the blood. Due to stress and tension, they seem to have no "appetite." Why is exercise so beneficial? When we run, our bodies burn more glucose in the muscles and produce more carbon dioxide, which enters the bloodstream. As a result, we become hot, the skin turns red, the pores open, and toxins are eliminated. It dilates blood vessels, improves blood circulation, and restores internal order. Eastern masters have a proverb: "If an ancient old man can hold his breath for 1000 heartbeats, he will turn into a young man." Of course, this requires many years of hard training and this advice is not recommended. We must act wisely and do everything within our inner capabilities. But even a very short breath-hold has a beneficial effect on the body system. When a person holds his breath, he plunges into inner peace, gains strength and begins to mentally contemplate, realize and feel the fulfillment of his words and feelings. And the power and name of God within him fulfills his desires. God created this world in His heart and Mind, being in complete peace and inner contemplation. Only in a state of contemplation and complete rest can a person hold his breath for a longer time. But at the same time, a person cannot achieve a state of inner peace and contemplation without also holding his breath for a longer time. This once again proves: without God we cannot achieve anything worthwhile. Only God made everything perfect. Everything perfect was created only by Him, through Him and in Him. He is our inner being and our "Life". We must be Him on this earth. He is the only One who has and can give us everything we ask for in absolute perfection. By making the wrong free choices, we mistakenly weaken our spirit and body. This brings us a lot of sufferings. We have stopped hearing the quiet voice of our spiritual "I am." But we hear the cries of the body, exhausted by impossible tasks on it, very well. The body screams at us and loudly calls for help. But we perceive these screams as our own negative feelings. By obeying and fulfilling them, we constantly live in suffering and pain. Obeying the cries of our tormented flesh, we worship and keep the commandments of a master alien to us, whom we have infused into ourselves, nourished with our vitality and settled to live inside our essence under a name alien to us. We mistakenly made the body our master. The body is not to blame, but our desires and the corresponding feelings and thoughts that we choose should be to blame. Thus, without realizing it, we serve not the True God of Love and Joy, but the god of suffering, illness and pain, an idol who cannot exist without our energetic help. This idol became our god. We did it because of our limited perception of reality and foggy consciousness. We keep it alive and active by feeding this idol with our vital energy. This idol is the same as those figurines of god-idols, made by human hands of wood or gold, which our ancient ancestors worshiped as true gods. We have not gone that far from them. The only difference is that this "god-idol" no longer lives in the outside world in the form of golden and wooden figurines, but was created and rooted in our life-giving spirit and acts as our second essence, the second master-ruler. We ourselves have placed it in our soul and store it there, supporting and feeding it with the low-frequency energy of our negative feelings, desires and thoughts. Our true Essence is Divine. How can this idol get food from us? As a part of the human body, it can only receive nutrition from what the person contains. In several previous chapters, we said that the human body is the soil into which desires, feelings, ideas, thoughts, words, etc. are sown. Now about this again in more detail. We are all the image and likeness of God. God has in Himself the fullness of everything, including male and female qualities. He, Himself, gave birth to the whole world and what is in it, in Himself and for Himself. Being His image on this earth, we also have the same qualities. In the spiritual body of a person there are male and female components capable to give life to any of our desires and fulfill them. If this sounds bad, sorry. But I think so. In other words, I think that both men and women, all of humanity, can be considered as "wombs" for the conception of our chosen desires, thoughts, words, etc. They are our spiritual descendants and therefore can be called our spiritual children. When there was only one spirit of the Heavenly Father in a person, a person gave life only to the desires of God. We could call them his and God's children. But in our time, there is another second essence within a person. So, if we choose what the idol desires, we give life to the "child" we conceived with the idol inside us. If fertilization occurs, a living cell of the desired child is born. If our desire in this case is conceived by an idol-liar and deceiver, forcing us to see, hear and understand everything distorted, then such a "child" needs food to grow and live. The Spirit of God within a person provides nourishment and fulfills everything that a person desires. The idol knows this well, and also knows well how to survive within us. He lies to us. Delusions make us suffer living in pain, surround us with problems and stress, causing negative sensations with low energy vibrations in the human body. After all, a child of a liar needs such negative low-frequency energy food. The liar, constantly deceiving us, provokes us, the Sons of God, to feed him and his spiritual children with negative experiences, those that have low-frequency energy vibrations, forcing us to suffer, live in pain, surround us with problems and stress. After all, the child of a liar needs such negative low-frequency energy food. The idol, in addition to feeding on our negative emotions, also feeds on our intellect. In fact, we give ourselves to him as food. The essence of God, our true nature, gives life to any human desire, thought, word or image, be it good or bad. It is enough just to keep them inside for a while. Living in pain and dissatisfaction, we generate low frequency energy food for this idol. Not a single idol can live without this low-frequency energy food in the Divine Temple of the human body. Feeding and growing up within our body, this "child" takes root in our Divine nature, feeds on our Divine Spirit, and firmly settles in the human body. The "seed" of a spiritual idol planted in the soil of a person's soul is like a grain of wheat planted in the ground, takes root in the Divine Essence of a person and, like a child in a woman's womb, feeds on the life-giving power of our Divine nature. We, without realizing it, voluntarily give this "parasite child" food to make him stronger. Feeding on our life force, the idol becomes "alive", as if in some semblance of God, and acquires the ability to create living parasitic organisms in its image and likeness - viruses, bacteria, fungi, and so on. Feeding them with its low-frequency "living" energy, the idol, with the help of these parasites, deceives and manipulates us. These parasitic organisms are the servants (or children) of the idol. They poison people with the toxins of their life activity and thereby destroy the internal systems of people, forcing us to live in suffering, pain and dissatisfaction. At first it seems that it is parasitic organisms who create our diseases and all other troubles. But they are only a consequence of our desires, feelings and thoughts in our hearts and minds. We constantly feed our idol-god with negative energy and, doing that, we support and strengthen it. By feeding on our true Divine nature, the idol weakens our Divine Spirit and greatly enhances its own spiritual power. Thus, humanity squanders its spiritual wealth and sinks deeper into darkness, becoming servants of evil. Misconceptions "live" in our minds and souls. To turn off the tap of energy food for the idol-god, we need to get rid of negative feelings, emotions and thoughts. Less food for the idol means less food for his servants. After some time, without food, they can dissolve and disappear altogether. Of course, this is not easy to do, but it is still possible. Moses believed that the leading cause of "blindness, deafness and misunderstanding" of people is evil in every person and society as a whole. At the present time, mankind lives according to the precepts of the idol, treating everything within themselves and on this earth as a ruthless planter treats his mercenaries. The free choice of desires allows us to act on this earth as the worst evil, the superior good, like God, or something in between. How often do we today violate the moral principles of the Ten Commandments, given to us in sacred books and written in our hearts, serving evil? I am not saying this to accuse anyone of anything. This happened. But it would be great to somehow change this situation. The fifth commandment of God, given to people for a pleasant and happy life, says: *"Honor your father and mother; May your days be long in the land which the Lord your God is giving you"* (Exodus 20-12).

The Earth is our Great Mother. Why? A mother is the one who gives birth to her children and feeds them with the milk of her breast. Everything on earth came from the Earth body. She loves us with unchanging maternal Love not paying attention to our lousy attitude towards Her. She feeds us "with the milk of Her breast." We do not open our eyes wide enough to see that the Earth is not a dead body, but a great living Being, a huge living organism with feelings and limitless intelligence. We mindlessly destroy the body of Mother Earth for the sake of money and a comfortable life. We do the same with the sky, where our Heavenly Father lives. Scripture says: *"And do not call anyone on earth your father," because you have one Father, and He is in heaven "* (Matt. 23-9).

This means that we all are children of our great Heavenly Father. Constantly breaking the rules of life, behaving like naughty children, we risk being expelled from this Earth. Eliminating wrong desires and ideas from our consciousness means we can live longer and better. Since a computer has a "delete" option, every person (and every creature) should have the same option. After all, a computer is created in the image and likeness of man and the Universe. Our life circumstances can change for the better only after a corresponding change in our internal energy system. We should all be like Jesus Christ, be God on this earth and not anyone else. The washing machine cannot operate as a passenger car. Man also should not and cannot function otherwise than to be God on this earth. Its inner workings and structure are designed to function only as God. Having severed the connection with God, man, having a Divine nature, managed with great difficulty to make himself not what he was and should be in reality. And this all happened because one day he saw himself as a body, separated from all other forms of the whole world and God. Believing his eyes and calling himself a name that did not correspond to his nature, he began to obey only his bodily desires. Because of this, he had to travel a lot in unfamiliar foreign countries. This path was not intended for him and cost him a huge loss of mental, physical and spiritual strength.

Let's have a look at another simple example. If for some reason we decide to use a passenger car as a washing machine, then, even with groans and squeals, it will not wipe the dirt from the clothes. Its internal design and construction are not designed for this. It's the same with humanity. The wrong borrowed name has deprived humanity of the extraordinary life that God has prepared for us. And now we, groaning and tormented by terrible circumstances, not knowing how to escape their grip, sell ourselves into slavery for the sake of material wealth, prestigious positions and some power over our brothers. Thus, we continue to destroy our inner self, conscience and moral principles written in the heart of every person moving further and further away from our great destiny. We identify ourselves not with who we really are, but, so to speak, with a washing machine, which we cannot be and cannot do its job (and should not). Errors feed humanity not with food intended for the Sons of God, but with a false idea, food fit only for pigs, as the Bible says. Food, both material and spiritual, fills the essence of a person and determines his condition. As a result, we often behave not as we should, but as evil, not only against ourselves but against the whole earth. But our mission and goals are to be good, kind and loving. We are born to obey no one and nothing except God. Our true nature is still ours. It's in our blood.

According to Eastern philosophy, everyone who wants to fulfill their true destiny must follow the path of spiritual development. To achieve a result, a person needs to go through two stages. The first is to unite all internal structures into a single organism to help the body vibrate in unison with its spiritual divinity. The second step is to separate thoughts from feelings and emotions. At first glance, this division into stages may seem strange. But upon closer examination, one cannot but agree with this. So, the first stage, as I understand it.

All information about oneself, the true and false "I", is stored inside each person. In modern man there are, as it were, two different beings, two masters who rule over him. One, Divine, kind and creative; the other is evil and destructive. The first, kind and creative, should become the basis of our lives. But, unfortunately, the information about Him stored within us often turns out to be unclaimed, forgotten and seemingly non-existent. Currently, all of humanity lives under the rules of the second master, who is a liar and deceiver, forcing people to see, hear and understand things in a distorted form. I think that today almost all people and the entire society are infected with deception. The liar and deceiver holds humanity and the whole world in his tenacious grip. And all this happened because a person, deceived in his vision of himself and the world, called himself a name that, in its characteristics, did not correspond to his true nature. This name now tries to change the Divine nature of man, breaks our relationship with each other, with our Mother Earth, Heavenly Father and makes us so spiritually weak that people, making great efforts to eliminate negative feelings and thoughts, cannot do this. At the same time, as the master of lies grows stronger, he begins to emit rays of hatred and aggression from the very center of humanity, just as the sun emits rays of light and heat. Thus, humanity becomes a source of hatred and aggression. These rays of evil enlarge and expand man through his actions in the material world, expanding and enlarging the body of evil. Under such guidance, the human body and the spiritual Divine "I am" work inharmonious. Humanity, by its origin, has infinite power and authority on this earth. Man has the power to give sight to the blind, hearing to the deaf, strength to the weak, stop earthquakes, calm storms, bring peace where there is war, etc. We are here on earth to rule the world, to be good and kind manifesting ourselves as God and desire only that what He desires. We were created on this earth to do His work with Him and for Him. He lives in us and through us. We are alive only because of His life in us. He created man in order to accomplish His purposes on earth through him and with him. Our purpose in life should be to be Him on this earth. One example. Man made a car to transport people and goods. The car's design suits its purpose. It was created to serve a person for movement. But if for some reason the machine itself or its owner decided to use it as a washing machine and filled it with detergents instead of gasoline, then no matter what buttons and pedals he pressed, the machine will not wash clothes. This is a vehicle for transportation. It is not intended to be used as a washing machine. It has a different design. Its design suits its purpose. It's the same with people. God created man with a unique design. Its structure corresponds to specific goals. We can and must do what is laid out in our program by its Creator. Therefore, all words, thoughts, desires and dreams that are not written into our system by the Creator pollute us, just as washing powder pollutes a car. Spiritual sages say that the first step is to cleanse the body of wrong words, desires, emotions and thoughts, like a car from "washing powder" and, as a result, from toxins and all the chemicals that we use.

The second stage, as sages say, is more difficult. At this stage it is necessary to separate thoughts from feelings and emotions. Why? How to live without emotions? When, in the first stage, man somehow reaches a spiritually perfect state as the "Christ-man," then, I think, the essence of man becomes a unified system. But information about past tastes and habits is still stored in his memory. As long as this old information exists, even the "Christ Man" can, under certain conditions, succumb again to old feelings and desires. Moses led his people through the desert for forty years hoping that after spending a longer time among pure nature and in the presence of the cloud of God, which showed them the right path and fed them with bread from heaven, they would forget their old habits and desires and begin to desire only everything that is true. God said to Moses: *"Behold, I will rain bread from heaven for you; and let the people go out and gather daily as much as is necessary for the day, that I may test them whether they will do according to My law or not"* (Exodus 16:4).

God took care of them and gave them bread, helping them survive and develop spiritually in the desert. The Israelis loved God. They promised to obey and keep all His Commandments and Laws. But one day the congregation of the children of Israel rebelled. They wanted meat, the food they ate when they were enslaved people in Egypt. After all, information about the past (they were in Egypt for 400 years) remained inside them. The information from the past can easily surface and manifest with great force. God, fulfilling every desire of man, sent them meat to eat. A huge number of quails dotted the entire field. After eating what they loved in a past, many of them fell ill and many died. The recollection of some former desires, feelings, emotions and habits when a person was not free, can again capture a person in a vice. Most of those who were born in slavery have not been able to completely free themselves from the habits and attachments of their former lives. Losing hope that his people would not be able to forget the old, Moses said that only those who knew nothing about slavery in Egypt and who were born in the desert can reach the Promised Land. A person who has reached the state of a "Christ-Man" will also have to go through the second stage of spiritual development - to learn not to succumb to the old feelings and desires that he had in the past. Everyone has to learn to turn off the thought from the former feelings and emotions that he had in slavery. Our bodies are liquid media such as blood, lymph, etc. All information is recorded and stored in an inner matrix. Every look, smell, desire, experienced feeling, emotion, joy or pain is contained in it and, one might say, determine our destiny. Some of the past experiences through smell, touch, or whatever happened to the person in the past, can come to the surface and push the one to feel it just as much as they did in the past. All desires, feelings, emotions and habits of a person he had in a past immediately begin to receive "living food" from the energy of a person's thought and become stronger in our internal system. They can once again put down strong roots in our Divine essence, just as plants planted in the soil take root and feed on it.

There are no boundaries between the first and second stages of spiritual development. They are conditional. But separating thoughts from feelings and emotions is necessary. We should not give thought energy to our negative feelings and emotions. People can do this only through volitional control and internal effort. To separate thoughts from negative desires, feelings, sensations, beliefs, memories and emotions is possible if harmful desires and feelings do not receive energy food from the mind. They cannot long exist in our divine essence without our active feeding them with our thoughts. When thoughts through volitional control switch to something good, "negatives" disappear. But if these "negatives" have already had rooted in our divine essence, then getting rid of them will be more difficult. It can be done only through conscious volitional control by switching "bad" ideas, norms, and desires to "good" ones that exist in the kingdom of heaven. Only in this way can one achieve the state called in scriptures "Christ, the Son of God." If a man has done it, no single temptation of the outer world can defeat him. He becomes in the likeness and image of God.

Jesus Christ told us not to resist evil with violence. I think he said it not only to stop the exponential progression of evil but also to our realization that every person we know or do not know is part of the same living spiritual organism of the Universe. For example, look at the breath. We all breathe the same air wherever we are, in America, China or Africa. Air masses are constantly moving from one continent to another. When a person walks down the street or is in a room with several people, each exhales air from his internal system, enriched by his energy information of himself. The mixed air exhaled by everyone is inhaled by every person with all the informational details on everyone. We breathe each other in. Thus, we are one body through breathing. Each man is a small cell of one organism of the entire Universe (or God) and the image and likeness of this Universal system. That is why the sages of the East say: "Know yourself, and then you will know the whole world." The commandment of Jesus Christ: *"Love your neighbor* (including your enemies and everyone who is against you) *as yourself"* means that everyone, even those whom we do not know and who live in some other part of the world, is part of the Self, and every other person on the planet is "me" or "you" too. The work of the Universal organism depends on the coherence of the work of all its organs and cells and, hence, on the correct functioning of each person individually. The same is about the human body. The human body's work depends on the coherence work of each organ and the cells within it. If a person has problems with the liver, it means that the failure is not only in the liver, but also in other body systems. After all, they have to do part of the work that the liver can not cope with. This creates an additional physical and spiritual burden on other organs and cells, including the nervous system. Under stress and additional pressure, they shrink and "isolate" from each other, just like people. To get rid of problems in our body we have disconnect thoughts from the pain associated with them.

The location of the disease is not in the liver or other organs, but in the energy system. Pain in the liver or other organs is only a symptom of some disturbance in the internal energy system. We only need to turn off the tap of "life" for their existence: to separate thoughts from negative feelings and emotions. It's not that easy to do. But it's good to remember: *"for God, and with God, everything is possible!"*

God's electromagnetic induction

Electromagnetic induction is the phenomenon of the occurrence of current in a closed conducting circuit under the influence of an external alternating magnetic field passing through it. The English physicist Faraday discovered that the current in a closed electric circuit creates a magnetic field around itself. He concluded that the magnetic field could also act on a closed conducting circuit and create a current. After many experiments, he concluded that an electric current appears in the circuit if a closed conducting circuit is in a changing magnetic field. It occurs either when the conductor is placed in a moving magnetic field (using an AC source) or when the conductor is constantly moving in a stationary magnetic field. The strength of the induction current is directly proportional to the rate of change of the magnetic flux passing through the conductive circuit and the speed of the conductive circuit in it. The main areas of application of electromagnetic induction are a current generation (induction generators at all power plants, dynamos) and transformers. It is one of the essential laws that were created and exist in the Universe or God. This Law is active both in the entire Universe system and in all living beings. If we look more deeply into the nature and essence of the entire world, we can easily see that there is no other power than the mental power of God. It is the subtlest and most powerful energy in the Universe. Neither man nor science created ether, air, electromagnetic and gravitational fields, earth, sky, planets, sun, etc. Everything humanity created is based on what has already been perfectly created by God's Divine Mind. We often tremble and fear Satan or the devil, who is none other than our spiritual descendant. This "evil" exists in man and for him and does not exist in the world of True Reality. It robs us of spiritual strength and prevents us from expressing our true nature. I believe that the whole society and every person must take active measures in the fight against it, doing everything possible and even impossible. We must build our inner selves and the entire society in such a way that the "evil" that deceives us no longer exists. Moral principles and Laws of life, written in the sacred scriptures and the hearts of people, should be the basis of our lives.

Electromagnetic induction is one of the main Laws of God, which can help us build a relationship between God and ourselves. Let's look at shamans. Calling on God, they dance, clap their hands, stamp their feet and spin around in the dance. At first they make slow movements and jumps. In dance, their movements are increased and intensified to such an extent that they begin to jump so fast and to incredible heights that they cannot perform in normal everyday life. In such a dance they acquire the powers of providence and healing. Why? In this case, the Law of the Divine subtlest electromagnetic induction comes into force. The movement strengthens in them what now occupies their thoughts, what they feel and desire. After all, our body is a closed conductor of internal electric and magnetic forces and fields. We all also live in the electromagnetic fields of Heaven and Earth. When our thoughts are on God, we are in and with Him. We are always where our thoughts are. Movements, jumps and dances with God-centered thoughts strengthen our spiritual state. Movement in the electromagnetic field of God increases the flow of vital energy within the dancer. Many examples in the Bible show that people danced to express their great gratitude and love for God. Rhythmic dance fills a person with great strength. Miriam danced in gratitude to God for bringing the people of Israel out of Egyptian slavery. God opened the waters of the sea to them, and with the same waters destroyed all their persecutors (Exodus 15:20). King David, dressed in a simple linen dress, danced in front of God's Ark of the Covenant as the people carried it from captivity to Jerusalem. He jumped and twirled around so much that his wife ridiculed him for it and said that he was simply stupid (Chron. 15:29). But David didn't care. He knew well and felt the great blessing he received by dancing before

God in His honor. Man has been dancing since the first days of his creation. Animals also dance. Dances, music and songs are the oldest forms of conveying feelings, emotions and information. On all holidays people always dance. To have fun means to dance. Dancing

enhances the feeling of fun and joy. This is God's law of electromagnetic induction. The Bible says, *"...a time to be sad and a time to dance..."* (Ecclesiastes 3:4); *"...and rejoice before the Lord your God, you and your son, and your daughter, and your servant, and the Levite who is at your gates, and the stranger, and the orphan, and the widow, who are among you in the place that he chooses. The Lord your God, and his name will be there..."* (Deuteronomy 16:11,14). Joy caused by alcohol is contrary to God. Dancing with the feelings such as pride, envy, jealousy, anger, and more of that type in the heart and mind increases evil and leads us astray. So, let's praise the Lord our God and dance in His honor!

Love and sex

The relationship between a man and a woman these days is increasingly referred to us as "sex" rather than "love." Being "sexy" is a big compliment, saying that a person is very attractive to the opposite sex. Such "attractiveness", of course, is. The energy fields of men and women are attracted to each other. The body of a man and a woman and their internal contents are a community of a wide variety of electromagnetic energy systems that harmoniously interact with each other. The act of "physical intimacy" causes both participants a strong feeling of euphoria, happiness, and joy. Such exhilarating sensations do not last forever, only for a short time. After an orgasm, a woman, overflowing with happiness and joy, shines with her whole being and flies like a bird, feeling nothing but bliss, kindness, and love. A man temporary forgets his plans and ambitions and becomes so kind and generous as never happens in everyday life. Why? That's why, I think. Man and woman are, first of all, spiritual beings, two unequally divided halves of the same fullness of the spirit of God. Both of them have their own unique qualities. Every person, whether man or woman, strives to find the missing part of themselves and connect with it in order to feel whole again. Having found each other, a man and a woman feel happier, but not always in the way they expected. The integrity of the Spirit of the first man on earth was unevenly divided between man and woman, endowing the woman with certain qualities and goals in life, and the man with others. Differences in feelings, emotions, dreams, spiritual and physical abilities, as well as the stress in which they live, prevent men and women from understanding each other well enough. This is why the love between a man and a woman is not what they expected and what they once felt when they were a whole Spirit and were endowed with that perfect love that we all dream of and which lives only in the fullness of the Spirit of God. Divided into two halves, they both stopped loving each other with the perfect love that was originally given to them. This brought disharmony into male and female desires, thoughts, feelings and actions. The Bible says: *"And the man* (about the woman) *said: this is bone of my bones and flesh of my flesh; she will be called woman: for she was taken from man, and they shall be one flesh"* (Genesis 2:23-24).

The merciful plan of God, who allowed the first man to be divided into two parts, a man and a woman, was that they would remain, as before, being in two fleshes, as one spiritual body, one whole spirit of God, as one undivided flesh. But that doesn't happen these days. The material world, tempting us, pushes both the man and the woman to become more and more independent of each other. From time to time, they both want to feel like a single body again, and then an act of love is performed. One body penetrates another, and for a while they again become one whole body, as it was in the past in the Kingdom of God. The act of mutual love, the penetration of one body into another first of all means the spiritual unification of the two parts of the spirit of God into a single integral Spirit of God. Man and woman, in fact, are spiritual beings, not material ones. When the two halves of God's Spirit unite into one integral undivided Spirit of God, the feeling of God's wondrous love, which exists only in the fullness of His Spirit, overwhelms them both.

The fantastic sensations that a man and a woman experience in the act of love arise only as a result of the temporary merging of the two separated halves of the spirit of a man and a woman into a single spirit. Experiencing a sense of "wholeness," they temporarily enter the Kingdom of God, spiritually uniting with and in Him.

Man and woman today are like the prodigal son, who, suffering in foreign lands, served there as a slave and all the time remembered how good it was to live in the house of his great Father. I guess that Adam and Eve, after splitting into two forms, functioned for a long time as one Whole Spirit of God. They didn't need proof of their love for each other. They both were always in this ideal love, like in a cocoon. And they both acted at that time as one integral spirit of God. Adam at that time did not need to think about procreation. They acted then as Gods, possessing all the attributes of God, including great ideal Love. The male and female components of the spirit of God between man and woman coexisted harmoniously in this great love. Both had such love that they did not need confirmation that they were one body and one spirit. Roughly

speaking, they were always in such a great
euphoria of love, which, as Eastern spiritual
masters say, often surpasses all other feelings
that a person can experience today, including
orgasm. Everything in God's world, in their
opinion, constantly lives in such euphoria that
it is even difficult to imagine. But since the
first man wanted to have a friend like him, he
voluntarily separated the female part from
himself and began to appear on earth in two
bodies, like all other creatures. As Eve began
to move further and further away from Adam,
their spiritual connection became somewhat
weaker. At some point, they weakened so
much energetically that both found themselves
outside the Kingdom of God. The man, being in
two separate forms, no longer lived as God,
but lived the same life as all other beings, from
time to time uniting with his wife into one
body in order to continue his material race.
Many in our time have turned this sacred
spiritual act of love between a man and a
woman into an object of only physical
pleasure, forgetting that love comes primarily
from the heart. First it must be the love of the
heart, and only then does this love result in a
sacred act of spiritual unity through the
physical union of two bodies into one. Biblical

scriptures say that a man has to care for a woman as much as he cares for his own body. It should be not only physical care but also spiritual. If he becomes careless of a woman's feelings, emotions, and well-being, this can stop both of them from manifesting themselves as one integral spiritual body. In this case, they will live and act as two different physical and spiritual bodies. Such relationships without the necessary obligations to each other, I think, are now called sex. The first man, Adam, was created as the greatest, unsurpassed being on earth, who was to bear full responsibility not only for the fate of himself and his chosen one, but also for the life of the whole earth. Today, unfortunately, he often behaves like an irresponsible creature. The same can be said about women. According to many great spiritual authors and scientists, the act of Love between a man and a woman is, first of all, a spiritual act of uniting two disparate spiritual halves of God into a single integral Spirit of God, where such feelings as love, happiness, grace, peace and bliss, which we can only dream of, live. The bliss experienced by people during the temporary union of two half-spirits into a single integral Spirit only reminds a person of the state in which he once lived permanently, and not temporarily. This is similar to the feelings of the prodigal son, who, while living in slavery, always remembered how good it was for him to live in the house of his great father. The great yogis, the sages of the East, the Christian Scriptures and, I think, all other religious teachings of the world say that the entire creation of God, every part of it is connected with everything else by the bonds of true love and, therefore, with God and lives in the euphoria, joy and bliss of this love constantly. Each of them is filled with such great happiness that people have never experienced either in everyday life or even during a "physical" act of love. Through a spiritual connection with God and His Love, a person acquires the fullness of the Spirit of God, which fills him with indescribable sweetness. Holy Scripture repeatedly speaks of the incredible feeling of happiness from being in the fullness of Spirit of God. *"How sweet are your words to my throat! Better than honey for my mouth"* (Psalm 119:103-104). Many other sayings from the Bible also speak of the sweetness of union with God: *"He is (God) sweet as honey; He who once tasted His sweetness will seek Him forever and ever;*

Its sweetness is such great that we can't even imagine it." The love between a man and a woman connects and fills them with the fullness of God's spirit. Therefore, they each become God for a while at the time of intimacy. He is *"sweet as honey. He who once tasted His sweetness will seek Him forever."*

King David was a singer who expressed his love for God through song. He also danced in His honor, no matter what impression he made on others. He knew the sweetness that he acquired from communicating with his Creator. *"How sweet are your words to my throat! Better than honey for my mouth"* (Psalm 119:103-104). So, he always kept Love for God in his heart. He knew well how great benefit he had from it. Constant connection with God overwhelms all being with the fullness of the Divine Spirit. King David knew well that it was the most to have fullness of God's Spirit in his soul.

Once in a newspaper one girl asked in her letter "What should I do? I am ugly and can't find a boyfriend." The answer was simple: change the image of yourself, and you will find a guy. And, I think, it was a great advice! People perceive each over not by the correctness of facial features or the beauty of physique but by the image carried and radiate from each person. Our thought or image is light energy. The intensity of this light determines which image is within us at any given moment. If we think we are ugly, we feed this idea and create an image of ugliness. If we believe we are beautiful - it becomes so. Our abilities, thoughts, emotions, actions, life, and destiny depend on the brightness (or strength) of the Divine Light energy we store inside. That Light (we can call it also our life) comes from the center of its source. The closer to the source, the brighter the light. Light energy decrease at a distance dissipating in a larger spherical space. At some distance from the light source, it gets dark, shadows form. There are areas where complete darkness reigns. This is chaos and an absolute misunderstanding of the nature of things. Everything depends on the energy of Light and the ability to "acquire" this energy. The intensity of the light (or Life intensity) determines our internal energy, as well as our location and distance from the light source. Thanks to our nature, we can work with ideas, words and images, transform them from invisible forms to visible ones and vice versa.

By attracting more Divine Light, we thereby acquire more vital energy and begin to see, hear and understand more correctly. But it takes some effort. Look what the caterpillar does. She isolates herself in a cocoon from the outside world in order to continue her race. The main task of a caterpillar is to turn into a butterfly and continue its race. Man, first of all, is a spiritual being. By living the life of animals, we give birth to our biological children, just as animals do. I believe that the primary mission of humans is to evolve into spiritual beings who continue their Divine spiritual lineage on this Earth. As we have already said, the Kingdom of God is so powerful that no one and nothing can remake or change it. But Adam, being God on this earth, still managed to change his vision and understanding of the world and his idea of his essence. Thus, man made the mental image of the world different from the real one. This world existed and exists only in human consciousness and only for man, but not in the Kingdom of God. Negative thoughts and a sense of "independence" from everything distort our perception of reality. The human body, I would say, is like a caterpillar's cocoon or an eggshell for the birth of a chick. In the world, we found ourselves, everything for procreation is born in a "cocoon", inside "leather clothing". Divine Alchemy of procreation in alien world to us occurs in complete darkness and isolation from this low energy world. While in this world, we may have several options: raise the level of internal energy and move to a higher one, leave everything as it is, or lower it, moving to an even lower sphere of life. Everything depends on our choices. Spiritual master Swami Sri Yukteswar Giri in his book "The Holly Science," described the seven kingdoms of the Universe and the same identical seven spheres within a man. The Central one, as we discussed it before, is the Supreme God Realm. No one can even imagine its power. But it's not bad to know that this sphere has unlimited power and is inside each of us and belongs to us. The second realm is the realm of Absolute Peace or the Realm of the Holy Spirit. It is also helpful to know that it belongs to us and is within us. The third sphere is the Kingdom of Spiritual transformation and Light. This is the Kingdom of the Sons of God. It is located between the realm of Spiritual Light and the realm of the beginning of darkness. The Sons of God, illuminated by direct rays of

Spiritual Light and reflected rays from the sphere of darkness, were abundantly filled with Spiritual Light. They partially reflected part of it, as I think, into the second kingdom of Light and partially illuminated the kingdom of darkness. They always stood, I suppose, with their faces turned towards God, seeing themselves with Him and in Him. The person held this role indefinitely. But one day, I think, the man turned around and saw the sphere of the beginning of darkness. An unknown, non-divine feeling entered his heart. The picture he saw was different from the one he had seen before. This touched his imagination. There was no God there. He could not see God. God was behind him. For a moment it seemed to him that he was completely alone, lost. And the desire to have someone nearby, a friend in the image and likeness of God, like himself, crept into his heart and thoughts. The Bible says that God fulfills all human desires. And God said: *"It is not good for a man to be alone... I will make him a suitable helper. And out of the ground the Lord God created all the beasts of the field and all the birds of the air. He brought them to the man"* (Gen. 2:18-19). *"But no suitable helper was found for Adam... Then the Lord God created woman from his rib... The man said, "Now this is bone of my bones and flesh of my flesh; She will be called the Woman because she is taken from the man. For this reason, a man will leave his father and mother and unite with his wife, and they will become one flesh."* (Gen. 2:20-24). It was not that that some Being in the form of some God came to Adam, took his rib, and made a statue of a woman out of it. It happened because Adam had the power of life in him, just as we all have it in our bodies. This inner Force saturates with vital energy any desire of the heart and mind of a person. If the desires are not God-like, they transport a person to an energy country alien to him, where there is no correct (spiritual) food, and different chemical reactions, some with +, or (-), begin to occur inside him. The division of Adam into two halves, male and female, could have happened not by the will of God, but by the will of man, who was His image and likeness. A perfect image of man existed, exists and will always exist in the flame of God's Love. But to be like God, our mind must work in harmony with His Mind. Since space and time do not exist for the Mind of God, they do not exist for people either. We, like God, are always where our thoughts are. The further our thoughts are from God, the further we are from Him. Our thoughts and desires determine our energetic saturation with God's light. God's light provides more than just the energy of life. It brings correct information, understanding, sight, hearing and happiness. The Light of God is the Light of Knowledge. It contains Absolute Knowledge of everything. This knowledge was, is and will be in each of us, in our internal systems. But the first man on earth, thousands of years ago, put this knowledge somewhere in the most remote corner of his soul and after a while completely forgot about it. Today we do not know what precious gift we have. If we could renew this gift, we would not need to attend universities or colleges. All absolute knowledge was, is and will be within us. Unclaimed, it does not manifest itself. Continuing to live by "their" mind, humanity retreated into the last and lowest sphere of Divine light.

The Bible speaks about the union of a man and a woman: *"The woman... was taken from the man. For this reason, a man ... will unite with his wife and they will become one flesh."* A man, Adam, for a long time loved a woman as much as he loved his body. After all, she really was part of his body. The woman revered the man as her master, receiving all knowledge only from him. Both of them for a long time felt that they were an inseparable spiritual body, and therefore they rejoiced in life and, having still the unshakable power of God, were happy. A strong distortion of their perception of reality occurred after the woman began to move away from the man more and more, becoming more and more independent in her thoughts and desires. It happened because Man became too busy with his ideas which were missing elements of a woman's spirit. That led to the fact that they lost the sense of the fullness of their unity and began feeling separated spiritually. Division of the inseparable spirit into two unequal halves weakened the vitality of each of them. As a result, they violated the commandment of God and ate the forbidden fruit from the tree of the knowledge of good and evil. That violated their inner chemical reactions more seriously and, as a result, perception of the real world and themselves. New vision gave them the idea that they were two forms separated from each other and God and were not in His domain but somewhere nearby. They both knew perfectly well that they had done the wrong thing.

Feelings of guilt and fear of punishment gradually settled in their souls. These feelings opened the door in their minds for a low-frequency destructive energy. They could turn everything back at any moment, but they could not do this due to a distorted perception of reality, considering it to be correct. Negative feelings gradually took root in their souls and, fueled by their Divine Energy, gained almost complete control over them after a while. Thus, a second "parasitic" entity was born in humanity, a spiritual "parasitic child" "conceived" from the ideas of lies. A destructive evil became "alive" inside them.

There are no separate spiritual forms of a man and a woman so that they can live their own lives and do whatever they want, not paying attention to their other half and the world around them. Man and woman have always been and should be one body (even in two forms) and one spirit and walk together hand in hand through everything that may come their way in life together, "until death do them apart," as the Bible says. Humanity is currently living with the idea of being divided into two "sex" halves. This is a misconception similar to the ideas of our ancestors they had about the shape of the Earth. The misconception about the division of one spirit into unequal halves has strong roots in each of us. It's not easy to get rid of this. A woman cannot cut a man's body and return to it. The bodies of two cannot become one body except during physical intimacy. But spiritually, with a strong desire, everything is possible. Each person, whether man or woman, can become a single harmonious spiritual being, as Adam was before his catastrophic fall, by restoring his Spiritual Divine Essence, drawing it from the Universe. By an effort of will, both man and woman have everything in their internal system to return to that image where everyone, man or woman, is the image and likeness of God. Adam did not realize that his ideas, after appearing in two forms, were incomplete, lacking the Divine Spirit imparted to Eve, without her love and sensitivity. This pushed humanity towards war, murder and aggression and ultimately influenced its attitude towards women. At first he dominated her, feeling boundless love for her. Later, weakened spiritually, his feeling of love for Eve weakened somewhat. He no longer had the strength to love his wife Eva so boundlessly and guide her in everything in life.

After all, most of the love went to the woman. Woman, as a part of the body and spirit of Adam, was, like him, the image and likeness of God. Without sufficient attention from "her Lord" Adam, she began to independently observe the world and expand her own knowledge about it. After all, she, too, as a part of Adam, had a Divine nature and was half (albeit a smaller, but no less important) part of God on earth. And she independently began to receive the Divine Spirit directly from their common Heavenly Father. The woman has now become so independent that she does almost all the same work as her "former master." The man also had to take on responsibilities that he had previously assigned to the woman. This is the process by which a man and a woman acquire the missing qualities of the Spirit that they once lost. But "qualities" alone are not enough. To turn off the tap of false ideas, men and women need to constantly fill their spirits with the Light, Life and Love of God. Moses gave his people advice that could help them see, hear, and understand:

"See, today I offer you life and prosperity, death and destruction. For today I command

you to love the Lord your God, to walk in His ways, and to keep His commandments, ordinances, and laws; then you will live and grow, and the Lord your God will bless you in the land you enter to possess" (Deuteronomy 30-15-16).

These are such simple words. However, they contain complete information for people on how to "live" life, to be alive and not half-dead.

*"On this day I call heaven and earth to witness against you, which I have offered you life and death, blessings and curses. Now choose life so that you and your children can live and love the Lord your God, listen to His voice, and hold fast to it. **For the Lord is your life**, and He will give you many years on earth..."* (Deuteronomy 30:19-20).

These simple words contain all the information we all need. God in reality is Life, Life giver. The body is just a tool for its owner "I am God". God is the only one who has and gives life to everything. Thus, "God" is the only truth. The whole World was, is and will be a single perfect organism of which each of us is a part.

Death and Life

Death! What a terrible word! Nobody wants to die. Even in pain, suffering, we cling to life. Every living soul longs to be, to exist, to be aware of its life and to enjoy its existence. After all, death seems to be something terrible! Non-existence and emptiness! Can it to be true? Does non-existence and emptiness exist in nature at all? After all, everything created by the nature of God is in a continuous cycle of life. For example, the water cycle. Ice turns into water when heated. Water under the influence of heat evaporates and already exists in the form of steam, forming clouds. Clouds, again, under certain conditions in the form of rain or snow spill onto the ground. At sub-zero temperatures, water becomes ice, and the whole circle of transformations of one form of the same substance into another, repeats. The same thing happens in the plant's world. Let us have a look at the grass. It grows out of the earth, feeding on its juices. Part of it goes to feed animals and, processed and saturated with the vitality of animals, returns to the soil in the form of excrement and excretory substances, where it is again processed into the same soil from which the grass grew. The life force that has gone from the earth into the grass returns to it multiplied as a result of its saturation with the life force of hay and animals. Everyone knows that animal waste is an excellent fertilizer that improves the vitality of the soil. Dried grass turns into earth, restoring it strength and the chemical elements from which it was formed. As a result of rotting, dry wood returns to where it came from. The scriptures say the same thing: *every end is a new beginning.* Everything in nature has a life cycle without beginning or end. But what is happening to humanity? We know we are dying. Death scares people. It seems that this is the complete end and we will no longer exist. But here is what philosophers, spiritual educators and teachings say about death. Yoga and Eastern philosophy say that there are two systems of nerves in the human body: voluntary and involuntary. A person, at his own discretion, can include voluntary nerves in the work, and when tired, he naturally falls asleep without any additional factors. This gives them complete rest. The voluntary nervous system rests during sleep, gains strength, and recovers. The involuntary system of nerves does not depend on the will of a person and works without rest throughout his life from the day of his birth. A person does not stop breathing day and night. His heart also does not stop beating and supplying nutrients and oxygen to every cell of the body day or night. But the involuntary nervous system also gets tired. When she gets tired, she naturally, like we fall asleep at night, also falls asleep. It called in their terms the "great sleep." This "great sleep" people call death. When the involuntary nervous system falls asleep, all the work of internal organs, such as blood circulation, respiration, and all other human body functions controlled by involuntary nerves, stop working. The body then decomposes and turns into earth. When the involuntary nervous system gets enough rest, it wakes up and the "great sleep" ends. The involuntary nerves awake in the most natural way, as naturally as we wake up from everyday night's sleep. And then the person (the one who was dead for us) wakes up in a new body with all unfulfilled desires and karmic information. But it turns out that a man still has some opportunity, to some extent, to learn how to give some rest to the involuntary nervous system during his/her life. The most important systems controlled by the involuntary nerves are respiration and blood circulation. Therefore, breathing exercises (pranayamas), according to yogis, with temporary breath holding and immersion of consciousness deep inside, help to give rest to these nerves and prolong the life cycle in the same body. Yogis also advise us to practice asanas, body postures that strengthen internal systems, including the heart and blood circulation. Among their exercises is a common pose for resting the involuntary nervous system called the "corpse pose." Of course, you can say that most of all I talk is about the yogis and sages of the East... But all their teachings, if you look closely, do not differ from the teachings of Christian scriptures (and, I think, all other religious teachings). Perhaps the forms of the statements are slightly different, but the essence is the same. Some biblical quotes also talk about the "great sleep" and awakening from it. Let's start with the Old Testament. *"Thy dead shall live; dead bodies shall rise!"* (Isaiah 26-19). New Testament: *"Truly, truly, I say to you, the time is coming, and it is already here, when the dead will hear the voice of the Son of God, and when they hear, they will live"* (John 5-25). In the above statement John conveys to us the words of Jesus Christ. Here is another saying of Jesus Christ, handed to us through John: *"For as the Father has life in himself, so he gave to the Son to have life in himself"* (John 5-26). And here is the statement of Jesus Christ, transmitted to us through Matthew: *"And the tombs were opened; and many bodies of the saints who had fallen asleep were raised"* (Matthew 27-52,53). This is what spiritual sages tell us about life and death. So, like everything in the Kingdom of God, life has no beginning or end and goes through a cycle of transformation through life into a "great sleep" and back to life. Life is not the only one in this present body. The belief that a person has only one life and it ends with death is another deception of our perception of reality. We are reborn and return to earth until we are reborn spiritually with a correct understanding of ourselves and the world. We have to fulfill all our heart's desires in this grossly material world. Only when we stop wanting them and suffering from the impossibility of their implementation will we be free. Rebirth and return to the gross material world can last indefinitely. A person will return to this world, where there is a lot of suffering, pain and hardship, until he is spiritually reborn into who he is, into the image and likeness of God. It means we must be spiritually reborn again. Jesus Christ said, "You must die by the flesh (spiritually) to be born again."

All of humanity today is experiencing (this is just my conclusion) a gigantic spiritual pandemic. In such conditions, it is extremely important for each person to comprehend his true nature. No one can do this for us, but everyone must walk this path on their own. You know, sometimes miracles happen in life, for example, extraordinary healings or others. It happens, but extremely rarely, just like hitting the jackpot. The program to be in the image and likeness of God has not gone away or been erased in the inner spheres of man. The only difference is the intensity of the Divine Light (this means the intensity of the inner Life Force). This is why miracles happen in our lives. A person can press all the necessary buttons built into his program without even realizing it, and it can work. But the jackpot is extremely rare. Scientists and prophets of most faiths claim that this planet has the most favorable living conditions for the development and improvement of all beings. What a pity if humanity misses this chance! But spiritual teachers say something very positive about our future. They say that our Solar System is getting closer and closer to the source of Intelligent Cosmic Power, called the Cosmic Mind. According to their prediction, our planet Earth should approach the border of the beginning of a new era of Cosmic Intelligence around 2040. From this moment on, humanity will take the first step to enter a new era of spiritual development. By receiving more energy from the Intellectual Spiritual Center, a person will gradually, step by step, develop spiritually. At the beginning of this period and its further development, every average person will be spiritually enlightened to such a degree that, without any effort of will, he will begin to understand his true nature and the nature of the entire Universe. I hope this happens before humanity destroy the planet and all life on it. The biblical teaching and the sayings of many other prophets also promise humanity the coming of a thousand-year reign of peace, goodness and prosperity on this earth. But, as they say, man proposes, but God disposes.

"Evil" rules the world today. Some part of humanity, through evil, is trying in vain to compete with God. "Evil" is just a tool with which God, the only Real Being, controls the entire Universe and through it achieves His goals. The Bible says that even evil serves God to carry out His good and pleasing great plans, which we cannot understand and know without seeing far ahead.

In conclusion, I would like to say a few words about the same thing that we have been talking about all the time. Let's look at a medium sized magnet. It consists of many tiny magnets. All of them are the image and likeness of a large magnet. Under "normal" conditions, all the small magnets are oriented in different directions. One is focused on the nearby power plant, another is wondering how a cell phone works, and the third is somewhere else. The total strength of all these small magnets is small due to their disorientation, and the larger magnet does not have much strength either. But if you place a weak magnet in another, stronger magnetic field, you will see a different picture. When exposed to a stronger magnetic field, all the small magnets are immediately oriented in the same direction, and the entire magnet gains strength. This is exactly how the Law of Electromagnetic Induction works in the Kingdom of God. Man, like any creation, is a collection of many mutually harmoniously interacting electromagnetic energies. His strength depends on the orientation of his cells, and the strength of his cells depends on his desires, feelings, emotions and thoughts. By attracting the power of God spiritually, we can place ourselves in the electromagnetic field of the Great Cosmic Mind. After all, God, His Essence, is everywhere, in everything and is the only Real Essence in the entire Universe. Space and time do not exist for thoughts. So, if we say that God is within us, He is there. If we say He is around us, He is there too. And if we say He, God is also everywhere and in everything, and He is there. Thought is omnipresent. It can also be in several objects at the same time and has no restrictions. Nothing is impossible for thoughts. It is necessary to place in the Divine Essence not only your body, but also the owner of this body, that Divine Essence that is everywhere and in everything. By doing this, our spiritual strength should increase many times over. Jesus Christ said: *"Your whole life should be prayer."* We must constantly mentally be in the field of the great Essence of God. Without being with and in Him, we lose our inner spiritual strength in a low-energy world that constantly disorients and tempts us.

A few words about our coarse material world. Despite the wealth of spiritual knowledge, many of us often feel that this material world is the only real world in which we live. But if we close our eyes, it will disappear for us. It exists for us as long as we see it with our physical eyes. The physical body does not create light. We can see the world around only because spiritual Light that emanates from the eyes when they are open. Fullness of Spiritual Light is very strong. Meeting denser forms it passes through them and connects with their inner content. With such intense Light, we perceive the world not as forms separated from each other, but as a whole single organism. If the light is weakened, then it does not have enough strength to break and pass through the dense shell of a separate form. It, reflected from a denser surface, returns through our eyes inside us, where the picture of the world is perceived as disparate forms, separated from each other. Our life is not in the outside world, but inside. We have to know the world by our feelings. We must learn to redirect and distract our attention from the external world, which scatters our strength and spiritually weakens us, to the center of the deeper spiritual realms and from there look with Him at the external world spiritually. Many spiritual teachers, prophets and scriptures talk about this. When a person embarks on the path of spiritual improvement, he acquires the ability to comprehend all objects and phenomena of the Universe not with physical eyes, but with internal feelings, and can transform the desired feeling from an invisible form to a visible one. For this, the sages say, the desire by it feeling must become so strong that the person himself becomes this desire and sees this desire with spiritual eyes as clearly as if he saw it with open physical eyes.

A person who has achieved such a state can have everything necessary for his life from God, and not through hard work. Then there will be no need for power plants, money, shops, etc. Then the Heavenly Father will take care of us like a mother and father take care of their newborn child so that the child has everything it needs to live in bliss, happiness and joy.

The Bible and holy prophets also warn and speak about hoarding. A person should not accumulate in reserve. This is contrary to the nature of God. God provides his creation with everything necessary for today. The manna, the bread from Heaven, then some of the Israelite had collected for today and for the days to come, had rotted and decayed. Accumulating anything corrupts the soul of a person and society. This is also associated with the accumulation of not only money, but also power and so on. Hoarding, whatever it may be, is a great evil both for the hoarders themselves and for everyone around them. Those who think only about preserving what they have accumulated lose peace of mind and stop living a real life. They live in internal and external war with themselves and others in order to protect and increase what they have accumulated. Their hearts, filled with love for accumulation, do not know any other Love, the Love of being with God. This misunderstanding destroys their souls and the lives around them.

We can go on and on about the same things we've discussed in this book, but ultimately it all comes down to one thing: we were created only for a specific purpose - to be God on this earth. Failure to complete our task threatens us all with being swept away from this earth. I think we are given freedom of choice for a reason. This is a test of our strength to be faithful to His laws and love Him in order to live a true life. The one who conquers evil is destined for the reward of Life. This does not mean that God gives it to us, but we ourselves must make such a Life. After all, we are Gods, co-creators of Life, and not evil and destroyer.

The Old Testament says: "You are the Sons of God." "You are Gods," says the New Testament. Yogis say: "The yogi knows God in the sanctuary of his Self." I would like to add that everything stated on paper or in books is just a theory. Practice is necessary. "God is closer than breath," says the Bible. He is with, inside, around us, in everything and everywhere! God, Life provider, is inside us. We borrowed the name "body" that was alien to us, but what we borrowed must be returned. This is not our own name. This name makes us weaker and takes us to a foreign spiritual land, where we suffer all the time. Our real name is to be Child (or Son) of God.

We are all great Spiritual Beings. Getting rid of the limited understanding of our nature and the Real World is the main task of humanity. Thanks to the free will given to us, we can do this. Choosing the right name with all its characteristics and manifestations means changing our destiny, yours and mine! Choose your great true destiny - to be God on this earth! Yes and Amen!!!!!!

Printed in Great Britain
by Amazon

38167118R00109